BEYOND FEAR

BEYOND FEAR

A Toltec Guide to Freedom and Joy

THE TEACHINGS OF
DON MIGUEL RUIZ

—— 25TH ANNIVERSARY EDITION ——

AS RECORDED BY MARY CARROLL NELSON

FOREWORD BY DON MIGUEL RUIZ JR.

COUNCIL OAK BOOKS

CHICAGO

Published by Council Oak Books, LLC
An imprint of Chicago Review Press Incorporated
814 North Franklin Street
Chicago, Illinois 60610

ISBN 978-1-64160-774-2

Cover design: Jonathan Hahn
Cover illustration: Nicholas Wilton
Typesetting: Nord Compo

The Library of Congress has cataloged the 1997 edition as follows:
Nelson, Mary Carroll.
Beyond Fear: a Toltec guide to freedom and joy:
the teachings of Miguel Angel Ruiz / by Mary Carroll Nelson.
        p. cm.
        ISBN 1-57178-038-6 (alk. paper)
        1. Spiritual life. 2. Toltecs—Religion—Miscellanea.
3. Ruiz, Miguel, 1952- —Teachings. I. Title.
BL624.N444 1997
299'.792—dc21   97-29355

                              CIP

Printed in the United States of America

PRAYER

Please join me as I begin with a prayer. First, read the words of the prayer and then take a few moments to close your eyes and do this little exercise yourself. Whenever you are feeling alone or without love, repeat this prayerful ritual and you will feel whole again.

Put your attention in your lungs. Feel the pleasure of breathing. To breathe fulfills the biggest need of humanity. When we fulfill a need, we feel pleasure.

Feel that strong connection between your lungs and the air. Just to breathe is enough to make you happy. You can always feel that pleasure of the strong communion between your lungs and the air. That communion is love. When the archangel created humans, he put a gift of love in the air for them. This gift of love fills all of your being when you breathe with awareness in every cell of your body, in every emotion of your mind, and in every piece of light that creates you.

Today, Oh Father/Mother God, we ask you to come to us and be always with us. We offer ourselves to you so that you can use our eyes, our voices, and our hands to share your love with yourself, because we are One.

In every direction from an electron to the stars, from matter to spirit, from every emotion to the energy of light, God help us to be like you are—to love with no conditions. Help us to love ourselves just the way we are, without judgment, because when we judge ourselves we find ourselves guilty and we need to be punished, and we suffer from the punishment. Help us to be like you are, to accept everything the way it is, to love the way you love, with no conditions.

Love is changing the whole world. Love is your real name and we are your children, so we are also Love. Oh, Father/Mother God, help us to be just like you are. Amen.

CONTENTS

Prayer v

Regreso a la Vida viii

Return to Life x

Foreword xii

Author's Statement xv

Introduction: A Dream Journey xvii

Chapter One
Teotihuacán, The Place Where Men
Become Gods 1

Chapter Two
The Vision of Teotihuacán 19

Chapter Three
Silent Knowledge and Elements of
Toltec Wisdom 27

Chapter Four
The Dream of Hell 49

Chapter Five
Mind, Evolution, and the Dream . . . 59

Chapter Six
Tools for Transformation, Part One
The Mitote and the Inventory . . . 65

Chapter Seven
Tools for Transformation, Part Two . . 79

Chapter Eight
The World of Justice................... 105

Chapter Nine
Life After Death....................... 109

Chapter Ten
The Way of Death at Teotihuacán........ 123

Chapter Eleven
The Ways of the Nagual in the World..... 147

Chapter Twelve
Gaya's Story—The Wisdom of a
Nagual Woman........................ 163

Chapter Thirteen
Prophecies........................... 187

Epilogue: The Cave of the Best Warrior..... 201

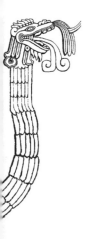

REGRESO A LA VIDA

Desparte, y ya no era el mismo
Por primera vez, abrí los ojos
Los mismos que creí tener abiertos
Engañándome por tanto tiempo
Sin saber que únicamente
Estaba viviendo en un falso sueño.

Con una hermoza sonrisa,
Como una estrella brillante,
El Angel de la Muerte,
En el Angel de la Vida cambiaba
Transformando de mis vida el drama
En la mas deliciosa comedia.

¿Es que acaso he fallecido?
Pregunté al Angel con sorpresa,
Muerto por tanto tiempo has estado
Y aunque en tu cuerpo el corazón latia,
Tu mente en la tumba de la ilución dormía,
Donde tu divinidad inconciente yacía.

Tu corazón aun late,
Tu cuerpo aun respira
Mas tu mente ha despertado
Del largo letargo del infierno.
Es por eso que tus ojos han cambiado
Admirando la belleza que te espera.

Tu divina concencia has despertado
De tu ser, el amor emana
Dejando el odio y el temor en el pasado
La acusación y la culpa han terminado
Perdonando tu alma has resucitado
Comenzando tu romance con la vida.

Mis ojos la vieron fascinado
Comprendiendo la verdad en mi dormida
Sin pensarlo, me rendí sin condición
Y ahora con humildad, acepto la muerte y la vida
Dejando ir las ataduras del infierno
Con gratitud veo partir mi amor eterno.

Miguel Angel Ruiz

RETURN TO LIFE

I waken
And nothing is the same.
For the first time,
I open my eyes,
These eyes of mine
I long believed could see
And find that all I knew as true
Was nothing but a false dream.

Then, like a radiant star
The Angel of Death
The Angel of Life became
And transformed my dream
From a drama of fear
To a joyful comedy.

So surprised, I ask the Angel,
"Am I dead?"
She replies,
"Yes, for these many years,
Though your heart beat on,
Your mind slept in the grave of illusion
Unconscious of your divinity.

"Now, with heart beating
And body breathing,
Your mind has wakened from hell.
Renewed, your eyes
Admire the beauty awaiting you.

"Your divine awareness wakens
All the love in your being.
Hating and fearing forsaken,
Gone are the guilt and the blame.
Your soul forgives,
Your divinity lives."

My eyes, in fascination,
Stare at the Angel.
Sensing the truth waking in me.
I surrender, willingly,
Without condition.
Humbly receiving
Death and life,
To hell, I release all claim
And with new eyes,
See my eternal love . . . leaving.

Miguel Angel Ruiz

FOREWORD

by don Miguel Ruiz Jr.

I met Mary Carroll Nelson in Albuquerque, New Mexico, in the winter of 1994 when she was working on the manuscript for *Beyond Fear*. My father, don Miguel Ruiz, and I were driving back to San Diego after spending my Christmas vacation at his and Mama Gaya's home in Santa Fe, and we stopped by her home to pick up the manuscript. She had been working on it for some time, and it was my father's turn to go over it to make notes and annotations. As brief as the moment was, I remember it with fondness because of their enthusiasm for the project. They both looked so happy. Along the drive back to my home, he told me that this book has captured his teachings of the past eight years, and that it will help so many people find their personal freedom.

Looking back on that day, after reading the book again after so many years, Mary Carroll Nelson indeed captured a very important moment in my father and Mama Gaya's journey. Their shamanic teachings were at their apex and the book acts as a time capsule of how they shared these teachings with their apprentices. The book is written from Mary Carroll Nelson's point of view as an apprentice, and it captures the lessons that her teachers shared with her, which allows the reader to experience those interactions themselves. We can even see the precursor teachings that lead to my father's first book, *The Four Agreements*, as well as the teachings that they shared in their power journey to Teotihuacán—teachings that are instruments of healing and personal transformation.

In contrast to the books my father later wrote about our family's Toltec Lineage, which are written in what he calls a "common sense" language, which is simply a language that we can all understand, *Beyond Fear* captures his teachings in the Shamanic Tradition of the Toltec

Lineage, meaning back when he used to teach as a Shaman. He stopped doing so when he began to focus on teaching Dreaming, the subject of his books henceforth. To teach as a Shaman is to teach through stories, metaphors, ceremony, and spiritual experiences, thus guiding the apprentices to their awareness of self, which is to go beyond the fear that held them back from living a life of personal freedom.

To go beyond fear is to come to peace with it and respect it, to no longer abuse it with our domestication or conditional love as an instrument that keeps us in an illusion. The function of fear is to keep us safe from real danger, but we can abuse it and distort it with our irrational fear, that fear we project onto life that is based on our conditioned beliefs and doesn't let us see life as it is. Thus, the illusion that makes us feel that we are safe only keeps us in a bubble that our irrational fear created. Through every step of our own power journey, which is the structure of this book, we are able to find that awareness that allows us to step out of such an illusion. It is the essence of the Toltec Tradition, the redemption of the parasite, which is our mind that has become the active domesticator in our life.

Mama Gaya, my stepmother, passed away in the summer of 2018, so for me to read her teachings in this book is something special to me; it is as if she is still here sharing herself with us. I didn't realize how much her teachings had impacted my own. I was always aware how her love filled my life, yet as I reread her passage, "Gaya's Dream," I see how her teachings helped me throughout my own journey. In essence the point of all this work is to heal the wounds that conditional love left in our mind and in our being; thus the concept of the redemption of the parasite, which is the redemption of the active domesticator in our life, is the moment when irrational fear, in the result of our domestication, no longer has a hold on us—bringing to an end our domestication, or conditioning—and we begin to experience unconditional love in our life, which to me simply means to love without any fear.

Mary Carroll Nelson indeed captured moments, lessons, and experiences that resonate after all of these years. Her experience as don Miguel Ruiz's apprentice, alongside Mama Gaya, during his shamanic phase of teaching, has been captured in this book, giving readers an opportunity to experience that journey for themselves. Shamanic traditions continue in the stories that the apprentices share in their own teachings—it is why we value oral traditions—but they stay alive in the actual application of the lessons that form said traditions. *Beyond Fear* is a workbook that sets up lessons, and the application of these lessons in life is what allows us to learn from this tradition. For that, I am very grateful for the creation of this book, and honored to now contribute to it with this foreword.

Thank you, Mary Carroll Nelson!

Sincerely,
don Miguel Ruiz Jr.
July 2021

AUTHOR'S STATEMENT

I t has been my privilege to know don Miguel Angel Ruiz, and his lovely wife Gaya, for several years. Miguel and I have shared numerous conversations in Santa Fe and Albuquerque, New Mexico, and in Teotihuacán, Mexico.

On each occasion I became aware, for the duration of our talk, that we had been in another dimension where the possibilities for transformation are boundless. In this other place, where Gaya also dwells, affirmation, a positive viewpoint, and a profoundly holistic sense of the sacred prevail. My task has been to collect, record and shape don Miguel's wisdom.

Though I am neither an apprentice nor a shaman, through the years of writing this book my imagination has been penetrated by nagualism with its eternal promise of heaven on earth, and I am grateful.

Mary Carroll Nelson
Albuquerque, New Mexico
May 1997

A DREAM JOURNEY

This book will take you on a dream journey into your imagination. Your destination is heaven on earth and your guide will be Miguel Angel Ruiz.

Miguel is a *nagual*.

Nagual is a word passed down from ancient times through the Aztec language, Nahuatl. The word nagual is making its way into English, particularly in discussions of shamanism. What is a nagual?

According to Toltec tradition, everything that exists is one living being, which manifests itself by creating everything that we can perceive and everything that we cannot perceive. This living being is the only one who really exists. All else, including ourselves, is an emanation of this great and wonderful being.

This being controls our planet by supervising the energy of the sun, and the sun also is an emanation of the one being, whereas all the planets orbiting the sun are emanations of the sun. All life on the Planet Earth is an emanation of the sun in an interaction with the Mother Earth.

To understand the emanations of the one living being, the Toltecs divided everything into the nagual and the tonal.

The nagual is everything that exists that we cannot perceive. We could call it the unknowable and the unknown. The tonal is everything that we can perceive with our common sense.

The tonal and the nagual can only exist because of intent. Intent is that connection or that force which makes possible all transference of energy between the nagual and the tonal. Without intent, neither the nagual nor the tonal would exist. There would literally be nothing in existence at all. Intent is life. It is eternal transformation and eternal interaction. Intent is what we call God. Intent is life by itself; it is God and it is Spirit.

In terms of our modern science, everything that exists in the world is energy. Light is energy and everything, at its root, is light. Energy has billions of manifestations, millions of different vibrations. The nagual is all the energy in the stars and between the stars that we cannot perceive. This is "el nagual." The kind of energy that we can perceive, and prove that it exists, we call "el tonal."

The solar system is a living being with its own metabolism, with its own nagual and tonal. The tonal is the sun, with all of the planets, moons, comets, meteorites, and satellites . . . everything that we can perceive with our eye and the instruments that give increased power to our eye. The nagual is the energy that comes from these planets and moons, including the energy that emanates from the earth.

Planet Earth is also a living being with its own nagual and tonal. It, too, has its own metabolism. Like the human body, which has many organs that work together to maintain a perfect equilibrium, the earth also has organs. Among these organs is the human organ composed of all human beings together. As an organ, human beings also have their own nagual and tonal. Emotions are energy that we cannot perceive, but we call them tonal because we experience them in our senses. The tonal in humans is the energy we know and also the energy that it is possible to know. The nagual is the energy that we cannot know with our reason. In the Toltec tradition, we call God "the Eagle," which means the spirit. All human beings are the Eagle. All human beings are the nagual, the tonal, and also intent, whether they are living or dead. When we refer to a person as a nagual, we mean that the person has a characteristic energy which creates a direct connection between the nagual and the tonal. The nagual can split emotions from actions. The nagual is born with a strong will and is not paralyzed by fear. A human being who is not born as a nagual is often paralyzed by fear. Nonetheless, in theory, anyone can become a nagual by intent. Some seers can see a person's characteristic mind energy in the energetic field that surrounds the human body. If the person is a nagual, the nagual energy field around the body has a shape like a double egg. The form is that of a mandorla, a slightly pointed oval.

A nagual is a person who has the ability to teach or guide others to the spirit by convincing them that inside of each person is a powerful force linking one to God. This is the force of pure intent. Usually, the nagual is the one who guides others to find who they really are, to help them find their own spirit, their own freedom, their own joy, happiness, and love.

Miguel Angel Ruiz was born a nagual. From the moment of his birth, he had a precocious awareness of spirit. He was an incipient Master of Intent. From a young age, he received training from his family and also through visions.

Miguel is dedicated to spreading his spiritual knowledge as broadly as possible. For a decade, he has drawn upon his visions to impart to his students a vast amount of wisdom that has been hidden for centuries. They learn from his lectures, workshops, and journeys.

For those who may never meet Miguel, the material in this book has the power to replace fear with joy.

We are all inculcated with fear. Miguel says fear is the normal result of our domestication in childhood. Fear is the root of the reality we usually perceive around us. Fear is the source of disease, of war, and of alienation from the joy that is our birthright.

The greatest fear, subsuming all other fears, is fear of loss or death. The path Miguel follows is straight into the heart of our fear of death. His wisdom is derived from a vision of the Toltec spiritual center in Teotihuacán where ancient masters discovered a process for ridding ourselves of fear. Miguel has journeyed to Teotihuacán with his students each month for years. While there, he has led them along the Avenue of the Dead. He has directed ceremonies at various stages of the path and guided his apprentices to confront their fears and to release them. From this process, they awake to a new view of reality in which the world is one of justice and happiness.

You do not have to visit Teotihuacán in order to benefit from Miguel's wisdom. It is enough that you lend your imagination to the inner journey of your own spirit.

CHAPTER ONE

TEOTIHUACÁN,
THE PLACE WHERE MEN
BECOME GODS

Teotihuacán, "the Place Where Men Become Gods," is the sacred center of the Toltecs, thirty miles northeast of Mexico City. The Toltecs retained and passed down through oral tradition secret knowledge of healing and spiritual transformation which remained intact for thousands of years.

Miguel Angel Ruiz is a direct descendant of the Toltec tradition. Through his heritage, he has an innate psychic connection with Teotihuacán. A former practicing medical doctor and surgeon, he received the spiritual training to become a nagual, or a Master of Intent, from his mother's family.

Who were the Toltecs? Miguel says they were not a distinct race of people such as the Maya. Traditionally, the word defined a group of people from a number of tribal groups who achieved a rarified level of spiritual enlightenment. They became known as Toltecs. Their elevated state of consciousness made them eligible to live within the sacred precinct of Teotihuacán.

Miguel recapitulates the history of Teotihuacán. He has learned the elements of this history through visionary journeys to the past and to other cultures. The story begins during the Third Sun, more than 20,000 years ago. At that time, there was a race of people who maintained a perfect equilibrium of body, mind, and spirit. Their immune system was so strong, illness was almost unknown. Science and technology reached a level higher than that of our present civilization.

Within that total race of humans—at least as large a population as today—there was open communication, and it was the result of an unrestrained communication within each human mind. Humans were not restricted by the concepts of guilt and judgment. The Third Humanity held in their minds a dream of reality that came close to being heaven on earth. It is remembered still as Paradise.

Humans are not the only beings with powerful minds. Attached to humanity are unseen beings who also are an organ of the earth. They share the metabolism of the earth, just as humans do. These beings form a spectrum from benevolent to harmful. Sometimes they possess human bodies. Many traditions are aware of them. They have been present alongside the human race from the beginning and have been called "gods" by various people. The destiny of these beings and that of humans is very close. The Toltecs called them Allies.

Miguel Ruiz:

The Allies lack a brain, which means they have no factory to create emotions, but they need the ethereal energy of emotions to sustain their life. Human beings are in a relationship to them much as cows are to people. We, as human beings, take in energy from sunlight through our food which is already processed by other living beings, such as plants and animals. Our brain transforms the material energy into the ethereal energy of our emotions. Emotional energy supplies food for our own minds and for the Allies or gods. We are just a resource for the gods.

Allies push humans to create traumas in order to create fear, which they feed upon. We are born with the disadvantage of being controlled to a certain extent by these gods through our dreams. The function of our mind is to dream. All of our life is a dream within a framework of matter. Dreaming gives us the sense of reality. We are born into a dream of war and violence. This is our challenge.

What if we all woke up? What would happen to the Allies if we wakened from the nightmare and found bliss? They would also have to evolve and eat love, not fear. Our souls already depend only on love and resist fear. In order to know if a thought is "of God," we can check to see if it creates fear. A fearful thought is not from God, although it may come from an Ally. The true God of love has nothing to do with fear.

To resist the coercion of the Allies, you must become aware of them. Even now, they are feeding on our emotions, so one should be careful what kind of emotions one is transmitting. Our emotions attract the attention of beings of a like kind. If we feel happiness, we attract more happiness. If we feel depressed, we attract depression.

Each nation has its own god. The destiny of humanity is the story of these gods. Jehovah is the god of one nation. Allah is the god of another. The identities of the gods are as real as the Israelis and the Arabs. When war comes, it is not just a war among people. It is literally a war of the gods as well.

Long before the building of Teotihuacán, the gods were afraid that humans could reach heaven. During the period of the Third Sun, the Allies became anxious for humans to produce more intense emotions, which they in turn could use as food. In order to achieve their own ends, they pushed humans to be more and more divisive. They did this by interfering with the perfection of human communication. The result was discord among nations. We find their destruction of world peace recorded in the Biblical story of the Tower of Babel.

The three major population centers then were: the Land of Mu, which we know as India and China (Miguel does not subscribe to the idea that Mu or Lemuria sank into the Pacific Ocean); the Land of Monkeys, which is North America today; and the Land of Atlantis, an island continent between Europe and America. For centuries, these nations had lived in harmony.

The destructive influence of the "gods" led Mu and the Monkey nations to join forces against Atlantis, which they destroyed in a massive nuclear war. (Here again, Miguel's viewpoint differs with those who believe Atlanteans were destroyed by their corrupt use of genetic power and the crash of a comet.) An account of this worldwide nuclear war is found in the sacred Vedantic scriptures of India in the Ramayana, the Legend of Rama. Miguel states that in the mountains of northern India buried remains of tall, strong humans from the Third Humanity are yet to be discovered.

A nation of people living on the northern half of Atlantis were pyramid builders. We know this nation as either the Titans or the Atlanteans, a dark-skinned race. Through their advanced system of communication, they were responsible for the building of the Great Pyramid at Giza in Egypt. Miguel says that the Great Pyramid is a monument to the Third Humanity.

Following the destruction of Atlantis came a time of decay in which the level of human life sank to that of an animal. In our present perspective, we are aware of only one evolution. We think we are an outgrowth of proto-humans. Miguel identifies our primitive forebears as the Fourth Humanity, the degraded descendants of the majestic race who preceded them.

The Fourth Human race were short-lived, sickly creatures of low intelligence. They lived their life spans of twenty-five or thirty years in such deep hell that they left hardly any history, but they were compensated by their prolific power of reproduction. The Fourth Humanity repopulated the earth after the nuclear war.

Here and there, on isolated islands, remnants of the Third Humanity held out for eight generations. These people retained their knowledge of science, technology, and spiritual development from before the war. They knew their time was limited, due to the effects of radiation. Since their power to reproduce was weak, they tried to use their remaining strength to teach those of the Fourth Humanity. They would visit the population centers of these primitives without getting too close, for fear of the disease that was so prevalent. Third Humanity people focused on teaching basic knowledge of agriculture and hygiene. Fourth Humanity humans thought of these taller, more intelligent beings as "gods." A memory of them can be found in sacred scriptures, for example, as the Elohim of the Bible.

Third Humanity survivors attempted genetic experimentation to improve the race. They also sought a way to retain the knowledge of the time before, when people lived in harmony and knew what it meant to have perfect equilibrium. Even then, the area of Teotihuacán was known as a sacred place. Some of the ancient wisdom was stored at that site for later generations to discover.

The Toltecs believe that the sun is the source of intelligence in the solar system. The remaining Third Humans prayed to the sun for help in safeguarding the knowledge of achieving perfect harmony. The sun responded. A new quality of energy came from the sun in the form of messengers. Light is the messenger from the sun. In this case, the new quality of light manifested as angelic beings who coupled with humans to begin a mixed race with the potential for a new evolution of intelligence. Enoch was among these mutated beings.

There is a belief among many current teachers and other wise people that the present generation of humans was seeded by beings who came to earth from outer space in spaceships. They claim that extraterrestrials performed breeding experiments using their own genes mixed with those of the protohumans. Miguel does not believe the seeding came from another planetary race. His vision is more mythic and seems to substantiate the possibility of virgin births, or of births stimulated by angelic beings sent from the sun who were not human. Whichever image seems to be correct, there is an element of "magic" to the mutation which altered humanity and led to our current race.

The change at that time in the sunlight that controls life on earth marked the beginning of the Fifth Sun. The Fifth Humanity—a race of mutants—is our own. We are partly celestial and partly of earth. To accomplish this mutation, the sun modified DNA to produce an improved human being with a better mind. The effort of the present evolution is to recover the perfect inner communication once known on earth but then lost, and the peace and harmony such communication produces. Once again, we are becoming aware of our human kinship.

We have rediscovered such concepts as peace, love, and justice. We have created laws. We are attempting to raise the living standard of humanity. Still, we suffer from our lack of inner harmony and we needed an influx of new energy to continue our spiritual evolution.

Since January 1992, the sunlight has once again changed. Its vibration is different and it includes more violet rays. We now find ourselves at the very beginning of the Sixth Sun. We are witnessing the birth of the Sixth Humanity. Forerunners of this new race are already alive among us. They know once again the basic dream of heaven on earth. All around the world, knowledge stored from the days of the Third

Sun is emerging. Many native traditions are releasing their wisdom while, simultaneously, advanced thinkers among scientists and philosophers are discovering concepts that lend themselves to a growing holistic movement. Today, there is a global proliferation of advanced individuals who have achieved mastery over their inner communication. Earlier avatars, such as the Christ, the Buddha, and Krishna, served as models. There have always been living masters, but we have been too afraid to accept their simple, single truth: We come from the light. We are of God. Once this truth is accepted, we can give up fear, self-hate, guilt, jealousy, and suffering.

Teotihuacán is one of the places where this ancient wisdom has been preserved. Miguel Angel Ruiz, while visiting the site, has recovered more and more of this knowledge during trance states. He believes his source is the rocks with which the various temples have been built. The rocks function like a data bank, and he has access, through his mastery, to the information left there by earlier masters. It was in one such trance that he "saw" the original builders of Teotihuacán when they, too, recovered the dream of heaven on earth from the site even before the temples were built.

Around four thousand years ago in the time of the Fifth Sun (which has lasted five thousand years), a group of spiritually advanced people who came from the north went into a cave which has recently been located under the Pyramid of the Sun at Teotihuacán. They shared a dream of a huge snake. One member of the group, Smoky Mirror, directed or guided the dream in such a way that the others would become aware they were dreaming.

Miguel Ruiz:

Smoky Mirror found a way to stop the suffering around him and to teach others to become the loving beings they really are. He knew that inner communication had been broken in the Third Sun, when humanity had reached its highest level. He was aware that a Judge and a Victim had been forced upon our consciousness by the gods. Self-doubt then destroyed our inner communication. Smoky Mirror saw that the gods are in a wrestling match with humans. They want us to stay in hell. The gods invade the human mind during the domestication process each child goes through. One of the troubling beliefs planted by the gods is "I'm just a human being." However, being human is not a limitation. The human soul is bigger than the gods, and the human mind is as immortal as the gods.

The gods try to instill a sense of injustice, which is like a knife that wounds the mind. Injustice creates emotional poison which is expressed as sadness, jealousy, and fear. The sore of the wounded mind can hurt. Once the mind is wounded it creates more poison. When others "touch our button" we feel the pain. We try to cover it and not allow anyone to touch our wounds, but this cover is a lie. It is like our armor, a mechanical system of denial and defense. We know that injustice is not fair and we try to touch others' wounds just to get even.

Toltecs were followers of Smoky Mirror. They were spiritual warriors who knew that they were in a battle with the gods who thrive on conflict. The warriors' purpose was to become gods themselves, to lose all fears and regain control over their own minds. To do this, they had to create love in place of fear. With this knowledge, they could shift the world to Paradise. Modern spiritual warriors are also aware they are battling against the gods who possess them. The possession is broken as soon as you declare your own right to dream your own dream. Free will can take you past personal pain and toward personal freedom.

Smoky Mirror discovered the primary wisdom left behind by the Third Humanity, that we are children of the sun. He found out that everything is made from light. We "eat" light and the light brings us messages from the sun, which controls life in the solar system.

Following the directions he received in his dream, Smoky Mirror designed and directed the building of the first temples at Teotihuacán. His wisdom was built into the very rocks of the temples. In later years, these structures were expanded and others were built. This group of magi, or wise people, founded a wisdom school, or mystery school, at this place where men become gods.

For several thousand years, the masters of Teotihuacán taught advanced spiritual seekers how to surmount fear and live as though they were in heaven, rather than the hell most humans perceive around them. In pre-Columbian times, the spiritual site was surrounded by a large population center of some two hundred thousand people. It was also the major marketing and production area of central Mexico. No one could apply for training with the Toltec masters. A candidate had to be selected. Moving incognito among the residents, the masters sensed who was ready to enter into apprenticeship with them. Without being detected, they applied different tests to determine the worthiness of those whose way of life they were observing.

When the masters perceived that they were nearing the end of the cycle of power in Teotihuacán, they were sufficiently elevated to do the same thing that scripture tells us Jesus did. They ascended. They left their physical bodies, became one with the light, and ascended to the sun. Left behind was a vacuum of leadership among the group of spiritual aspirants who were at various levels of learning but not yet at the stage of mastery.

When an invasion of barbarians from the north overtook Teotihuacán, the remaining Toltecs in training were unable to withstand them. Many died.

The barbarians intermarried with the people of Teotihuacán and attempted to adapt Toltec spiritual practices to their more primitive beliefs in jealous gods who demanded human sacrifice. The bodies that have been discovered buried beneath the Pyramid of the Sun at Teotihuacán are probably those of the spiritual seekers who defied the invaders and were ritually murdered.

Corruption overcame Teotihuacán. Around the year 700 A.D., it was abandoned as a spiritual center. Its temples were deliberately buried. Twentieth-century archaeologists are uncovering the site and making it accessible again in time to coincide on an esoteric level with the emergence of the Sixth Humanity.

There was an exodus of the remaining Toltecs in training from Teotihuacán. Some of them went south and merged with the Mayans who were at that time in a state of complete decadence. From that merger of the Toltecs and Mayans came the new Mayan Imperium.

Others formed a new community at Tula, where at first the knowledge of the Toltec masters was retained. Little organizations in the villages tried to preserve the knowledge like a religion. The villages fought for control. The high priest came from the most powerful city in the Tula area.

The high priest was considered the incarnation of Quetzalcoatl, the Feathered Serpent, who was one of the Twin Brothers. The other twin was Smoky Mirror. In the Toltec religion, these twins were the representation of the nagual and the tonal. They took turns carrying these two energies. At times, Smoky Mirror carried the nagual energy while Quetzalcoatl carried the tonal energy. Then they would reverse places.

The Toltec knowledge was eventually corrupted by the leaders of Tula who succumbed to temporal power. They misused the silent knowledge of Teotihuacán in their efforts to escape death. Miguel says some of the worst black magicians the world has ever known were there. They turned Quetzalcoatl into a demon in much the same way that later powerful Christians used the name of Jesus as a demon.

The Aztecs became the most powerful little country in Mexico. They built Temple Mejor in Mexico City and they tried to instill the wisdom from Tula. The Aztecs became the new Toltecs.

Two groups of spiritual warriors among the Aztecs preserved the Toltec's wisdom for five hundred years following the Spanish Conquest. They were the Jaguar Knights, who were warriors in training, and the Eagle Knights, who were fully trained naguals.

Jaguar Knights were initiated into death in a ceremonious ritual involving water and fire, during which they renounced fear, anger, and jealousy. After their training and initiation they saw the world in a new way, as a world of justice. They then became Eagle Knights.

The highest of Eagle Knights was the Tlatoani, the representative of God on earth. Any Eagle Knight could be a Tlatoani. Miguel's family were Eagle Knights.

The Eagle represents divinity. All Eagle Knights, even to the present day, are in daily contact with divinity. They are in a state of constant happiness. The practices they follow to achieve an awareness of bliss were also followed in Ancient India, Egypt, and Greece, and remain as living traditions among native people. In early times, Teotihuacán was connected worldwide with many other sacred centers. All of them shared the same basic silent knowledge.

The Toltec way of life promotes a perfect equilibrium of body, mind, and soul. In most traditions, some functions of the body are judged to be undesirable. Elevated spiritual warriors who follow the Toltec way are not required to be celibate. A basic tenet of their belief is to respect the human body as a temple, perfect just as it is. The effort of the Toltecs is to become fearless, without judgment, without victimization, and in a state of love.

Miguel makes frequent references to other traditions. He has a special love for the Bible and the story of the life of the Christ. He also reveres the memory of the Buddha. In his lectures, he connects the Toltec way to the lives of these avatars. All paths, he says, are basically the same, but the major religions have all been infiltrated with guilt, judgment, and fear.

The Lineage of Miguel Angel Ruiz

Miguel is the thirteenth child of famed healer Mother Sarita. During his early childhood, she was a locally known curandera, or healing woman. When Miguel was eleven years old, Sarita became seriously ill with gallstones. The doctors wanted to operate, but an underlying heart disease made general anesthesia dangerous. Sarita's mother took her to a familiar healing center for psychic surgery. During this procedure, Sarita had a vision of a doctor and three nurses operating on her gallbladder. She asked for them when she opened her eyes, but the only person there was the medium. The surgery healed Sarita of both her gallstones and her heart problem. Thereafter, she dedicated her life to healing others by using her inherited wisdom.

Miguel was brought up with an awareness that another dimension beyond the visual affects the material level of reality. His older brothers and sisters told Miguel of the times they had sat around the fire with their maternal grandparents, long before Miguel was born, hearing the stories of the little people who lived nearby. His siblings saw such creatures playing in the trees around the house. The town of his mother's birth, Juanacatlan, was a special place, what Miguel calls "a magical town." One of the town's residents, Don Nachito, owned the pharmacy and served as a substitute for a doctor. He liked to give gifts to children, especially gifts of money. "My brothers used to get money from him. He would make the money. He said to my older brother, 'I'm going to put a coin in this box. It's yours. Put it under your pillow. Every day it will have another coin inside.'" His brother waited to open the box until driven by curiosity, but when he opened it he found it was filled with coins. Hearing these extraordinary tales while he was growing up conditioned Miguel to accept that there is a magical level of life beyond the visible everyday world.

In his third year of medical school, Miguel had his own traumatic introduction to this other dimension during a violent car accident when he had an out-of-body experience. From then on, his inner visions accelerated.

Miguel graduated from the University of Mexico medical school. He then served for one year in the village of Alta Sonora in the Sonora Desert.

Miguel Ruiz:

It was a whole year of wonderful experience. I met frequently with a master who was a skinny man in his late forties, about 5' 5" tall, named don Esteban. He took me as his apprentice. He showed me amazing things and he taught me to go deep into the dream state and to explore the dream.

Don Esteban took me into a cave where he taught me a way to control the elements with an invocation. This is a powerful way to control the energy between life and death, a way to communicate with the different organs of the planet, like the wind, the water, and the forests. He made me face most of my fears. He always challenged my reason, challenged my intelligence, and mainly challenged my personal importance. He taught me the way to be humble and to respect everything that is, just the way it is. He taught me to respect nature and to respect humans, just the way they really are.

Don Esteban was a wonderful man. He was powerful, loving, and kind, but every time I saw him I knew he was going to challenge my fears. I always wore a defensive mask with him.

One year after I left the town, I went back looking for him and it was a big surprise to find that nobody knew him. No one had ever heard of him. It was as though he never existed. In those little towns, everyone knows each other. Then, I began to doubt in my mind whether he really had been born in flesh and blood . . . or was he just another state of consciousness in which I made him in the way I preferred him to be. Today, I understand that there was a close connection between my grandfather, don Leonardo, and don Esteban.

After serving for one year as a village doctor, Miguel joined his two older brothers, both doctors and surgeons, and established his medical practice in Tijuana in 1978.

In 1980, Sarita asked Miguel to begin an apprenticeship with her. Each Sunday throughout his intensive training for the next three years, he spent between eight and twelve hours in trance. In an altered state of consciousness he journeyed to ancient Egypt, Greece, India, China, and Persia and learned their belief systems. These experiences had the same vividness and authenticity as traveling in real life. Miguel's etheric journeys yielded such viable, authentic information about these historic traditions that he could compare them with contemporary Hinduism, Buddhism, Zoroastrianism, and Christianity. He concluded that all systems of belief have a similar core.

Trance Travel to Egypt

One Sunday during the second year of Miguel's apprenticeship, twenty-one of Sarita's apprentices (including three of Miguel's brothers) gathered with her and Luis. They were going to enter the trance state. The practice was familiar to Miguel. He had been trained by the old man who served as his teacher in the desert where Miguel served his year of public service as a newly graduated doctor. He moved easily into the dream state where he found himself in a long underground hallway. Although he knew he was dreaming, he had a vivid experience. In real time the trance dream lasted eight hours; in dream time it encompassed nearly a year.

Miguel Ruiz:

I was in the entrance. Behind me, I heard a door shut and I was inside a hall illuminated by torches. I knew from experience I could control my dreams as if I were awake. No aspect of dreams scared me, yet this dream was different. I was in another reality and I could not control it. This dream exists in the memory of the planet. It is available to anyone who has the training to enter it.

A tall, skinny, bald man appeared to me. He was dressed in a wrapped Egyptian garment of white cotton. He seemed to be fifty or sixty years old. Around his eyes there was a strong, dark shadow. He held himself severely in an authoritarian posture. I knew I would be tested.

Since I could not control the dream, I decided to be the Stalker. (This means I would have to be acutely aware of everything that happened to me and in me throughout the dream.) I opened my ears and determined to learn as much as I could from the man, not only from his words but from his attitude, as well. He was clearly a learned man. He impressed me. I could not play games with this man. He was very humble and serious.

Right away he tried to intimidate me. He was testing me. He asked, "Do you know why you are here?"

I said, "I came here to learn."

I was not sure where I was. I only knew it was a sacred place, a holy place where the intention was to find esoteric knowledge.

"Do you know where you are?" he asked.

"I am in a sacred place where there is hidden knowledge," I said.

"If you are here to learn, you cannot leave this place until you learn," he said.

Inside, I felt the words "to learn what?" although I did not say anything aloud. The old man took a torch from the wall and began showing me images on both sides of the corridor. This hallway of images still exists in ruins, but at a certain level of vibration it still exists in prime condition. That is the vibrationary level I reached in my dream. The same frequency can be found in other sacred sites in Greece, Teotihuacán, and Peru. We could say that the frequency is the same as that of the Christos, although that is merely our way of understanding it. A vibration is a frequency of light in the memory of light. Everything is light. Light has a strong memory. To vibrate at the same frequency as anything that ever existed is to access it.

I did not recognize the images the old man was showing to me. Yet, from the style of the glyphic figures, I knew I was in Egypt. Also, the man himself reflected what I knew of Ancient Egypt. In my mind came the words, "That man is a Hierophant."

The Hierophant said, "You must tell the meaning of these figures on the wall before you can leave. Don't be concerned about food or drink. Just try to understand." Then, he left me alone.

I tried to understand but I had no idea of the meanings of these images. Days, weeks passed. At a certain point, I felt a fear that I would never learn and I could never leave. Even though I was in a trance, it could not save me because I had entered someone else's dream. I was overcome by panic.

Something changed very quickly and I surrendered to the experience. I was no longer in a hurry to leave. I felt it would be all right if I stayed there forever.

I do not know how long I struggled before I surrendered, but suddenly, I started communing with the energy of the figures on the wall. Miracles happened.

Surrendering is a way of being happy in any circumstance. I accepted that place as my new world. Everything began to make sense to me. I was no longer concerned about time. I just accepted the interchange of energy as the figures seemed to come alive. A state of communion is a state of vibrating at the same frequency. I was not using my reason.

The Hierophant returned and I was sure that I knew the meaning of the figures and I wanted to tell him. I felt calm. But, he just smiled and said, "You may go." This was another test. I was not allowed to ever say what I had learned.

When I woke from my dream, all the group were already awake. They had been waiting for me for a long time. I shared my vision with them. Each person shared his or her dream too and wrote it down in Sarita's *Book of Life*. Later, Sarita burned the book.

This single dream gave Miguel a totally basic reference against which he could test everything else. He understood that the images on the wall of the Egyptian hallway were illustrations of *The Book of Thoth*. This ancient collection of wisdom is known by other names: *The Egyptian Book of the Dead* and *The Book of Hermes*. It is thought to be at least 35,000 years old.

Miguel realized that the images he had seen are the source of what we today call Tarot cards. For a time, Miguel studied the Major Arcana of the Tarot in order to absorb energy from the images. In his studies, he made the discovery that no set of Tarot cards is entirely accurate, but those designed by Pamela Coleman-Smith under the direction of Arthur Edward Waite are based in love. The cards designed by Aleister Crowley are based on fear. To check this out, try a comparison of the Fool in the two decks. The happy fool in the Waite deck is transformed into a monster in the Crowley deck.

From his understanding of the original Tarot, Miguel says that Judgment should properly be called Resurrection. The World is actually the Universe. Strength is more accurately named Courage.

The Tarot illustrates *Genesis,* and by arranging the cards in a certain order, one can see a similar structure to that of the Avenue of Death at Teotihuacán, which is the source of Toltec wisdom. You can try this arrangement yourself:

FIRST ROW	*The World* (Universe)
SECOND ROW	*The Magician*
THIRD ROW	*The High Priest*
	The Hierophant (Adam and Eve)
FOURTH ROW	*The Emperor*
	The Lovers (Paradise)
	The Hermit

FIFTH ROW	*The Empress*
	The Chariot
	Temperance
	Death
SIXTH ROW:	*Strength* (Courage)
	Judgment (Resurrection, Justice)
SEVENTH ROW	*The Star, The Moon*
EIGHT ROW	*The Sun*
NINTH ROW	*The Fool*

Miguel will write a future interpretation of the Tarot, but for our purposes, he says the Fool is Everyman dreaming that he does not know where he is going, while carrying all his attachments in his hobo bag. But, in his hand, he also carries the lotus of divine consciousness.

Outside the Avenue of Death, four cards represent hell. These are the Devil, the Tower, the Wheel of Fortune, and the Hanged Man. Inside the Avenue, the Sun is the archetype of perfection as in Ra, Horus, Hermes, the Christ, Krishna. Caught within the pattern are four cards that represent the Archangels. Ariel is the Lovers, and this stands for Fire. Temperance is for Raphael and earth. The Chariot is both Michael the Warrior and Water. The Messenger is Gabriel and also Air. If the pattern is looked upon as a glyph, it becomes the Eye of Ra, which is the Doorway to Infinity or the Doorway to God. The outer row alone is the double snake of Teotihuacán.

A by-product of initiation through the trance system is learning to see into the depths of symbols. Miguel has a profound talent for grasping the linkages among symbolic systems. He senses the Oneness at the root of all the esoteric wisdom that is being released to human consciousness at this time.

Mother Sarita was satisfied, following his apprenticeship, that Miguel was a fully trained nagual, and she declared him to be a Master of Intent with full control over will, spirit, and unconditional love.

When Miguel compared nagual healing techniques to allopathic medical and surgical curing methods, he concluded that his nagual energy made him a more effective healer. Although he believes some diseases and medical problems are best treated with direct medical intervention, he came to realize that conventional medicine was not enough to heal the sickness of spirit pervading this planet. After long inner debate, he decided to give up his medical practice and devote himself to his inherited tradition. This decision was not an easy one to make for it meant giving up the identity he had worked so long to achieve. Over the next four years, he taught and did healings at Mother Sarita's healing temple in San Diego, California.

Miguel lectures, conducts workshops, and guides meditations. He also leads journeys to sacred sites and gives counseling and healing in private sessions in Santa Fe, San Diego, Los Angeles, Sacramento, and elsewhere in the United States and in Mexico. The outreach of his work is steadily expanding. He has founded the Sixth Sun Foundation, an outgrowth of the earlier healing temple, Nueva Vida, which he built for his mother and has now closed.

"I am still working as a doctor, but I no longer heal just the body. My goal is to touch the spirits of people and let them know they have a choice," Miguel says.

Miguel's earliest contact with Toltec lore came in stories told by his maternal grandfather, don Leonardo Macias. Don Leonardo was also a nagual, but he shared his knowledge with only a limited number of associates. His daughter Sarita divulges her wisdom to those who seek her help. Miguel has always known, from the age of six, that his family expected him to share his family's knowledge as widely as possible.

Some months before Miguel was initiated as a Master of Intent, Gaya Jenkins consulted Mother Sarita for a health problem. Sarita suggested she attend the classes Miguel was teaching. As soon as Gaya walked into the classroom, Miguel recognized her as the woman from dreams he had experienced since his youth. She had the same boldly beautiful face, the same voice, and the same manner. From that meeting came the partnership and marriage of Miguel and Gaya.

Long before, don Leonardo had warned Miguel that the energies in ancient sites still have great power, and he told him not to go to them until he was ready. Miguel had never visited his ancestral site of

Teotihuacán before March 1988, when he took Gaya there on a sight-seeing honeymoon. As they entered the first gate of the site, Miguel and Gaya felt like ordinary tourists, but it soon became apparent to both of them that they were so affected by Teotihuacán they found themselves locked into separate, private dreams. Miguel's visions from that day initiated the rapid synthesis he has made of Toltec wisdom with sacred knowledge from other cultural traditions that comes to him more and more frequently in dreams and trance states.

In the following chapters, you will share the wisdom Miguel has received, which was formerly held secret awaiting this particular moment in history when all knowledge retained for centuries among native people is being revealed.

Prepare yourself to enter another dimension, parallel to the one you know from daily life, in which magic is a normal occurence. You already visit this dimension in your night dreams and daydreams, but you may not have been doing it consciously. To follow the Toltec path to freedom from fear, you will do as the nagual does. You will enter and leave this parallel universe by traveling into your own mind.

CHAPTER TWO

THE VISION OF TEOTIHUACÁN

As Miguel Angel Ruiz and his new wife, Gaya, sat on the peak of the Pyramid of the Sun at Teotihuacán, a vision unfolded in his inner eye. Looking to his left some two thousand feet away, he saw the Temple and Pyramid of Quetzalcoatl, the Feathered Serpent, and its forecourt. The plaza, he now saw in a flash of insight, is the head of a snake whose open mouth reaches up the steps of the temple.

Slowly turning his head, Miguel traced the "body" of the snake out of the plaza to the north where it joins the Avenue of the Dead. He looked down on this route 210 feet below his perch and followed its progress another three thousand feet to the Pyramid of the Moon on his right. There again, he saw that the plaza is a snake's head whose mouth is the steps of the temple attached to the front of the pyramid.

Immersed in his vision, Miguel suddenly remembered the dream that first came to him in childhood and recurred as he grew older. In this dream, he always felt himself being drawn into the mouth of a huge two-headed snake. It swallowed him whole. Beyond the ferocious head, the snake's body opened into a tunnel filled with demons. He believed that the tunnel represented the experience of death. Miguel sensed that he no longer had a body. He was only his consciousness. The deeper he went into the tunnel, the more his fears fell away. They were replaced by feelings of peace.

Miguel had this dream a number of times. Each time the dream returned he went further into the tunnel before wakening. Finally, he went all the way through the serpent's body and fell into the second head. He was then disgorged in a transformed state, deeply aware that he was a part of everyone and everything, completely connected to the entire universe. The dream had mystified Miguel, but he could now see that it represented Teotihuacán.

Another memory flooded his mind. Don Leonardo had once told him, "In Mexico, a giant snake has been sleeping for hundreds of years. Soon, a man of knowledge will awaken the giant. When it awakens, the planet will change. Humans will change the dream of the planet." This story also connected with Teotihuacán, and it seemed related to his dream.

"My dream was an echo of an ancient dream. I was attuned to this other dream which someone else had, that inspired the building of this place. This other person was Smoky Mirror. Smoky Mirror and I are one being, because I am connected to his vibration," Miguel explains.

All of us have a potential ability to contact the vibration pattern of anyone who has ever lived. These patterns of lives, called the akashic records, exist at an etheric level. Miguel's concept is that, by contacting a former life pattern, a soul reincarnates that pattern in itself. Our soul may not have lived as another person, but when we are in an altered state we can access another life vibration. By tuning into it, we reawaken a permanent part of our memory. Miguel reawakened Smoky Mirror and dreamt his dream.

Teotihuacán provoked such a profound sense of déjà vu in Miguel that he tuned into yet another life pattern. He saw himself standing in the Plaza of the Temple of Quetzalcoatl amidst a crowd of worshipers, people who had come from great distances faithfully expecting a miracle. The year was 1929. The self he envisioned was a Hindu monk wearing an orange robe. Miguel entered this experience just as the monk said to himself, "I am going to be born in Mexico to a family who will teach me the knowledge of Teotihuacán." In 1952, a few months after this monk died, Miguel Angel Ruiz was born. Therefore, his soul had entered Sarita's body prior to the death of the monk. This episode conforms with classical Eastern beliefs in reincarnation. It is not surprising that the event involves India.

In his present life, Miguel could be taken for an Asian Indian. He is a small man with wavy, dark hair. His face is animated by large, wise, dark eyes. It would be easy to imagine him wearing a robe or a *dhoti* at home among other Hindi. India has attracted him so strongly that he went there and performed a ritual death in order to sever his connection to that country and free himself to live his present life.

Miguel Ruiz:

I no longer feel I am from India. I am from this world now. The same ancient silent knowledge is available in India as in Mexico, but the discipline is different. In India time moves very slowly. It is appropriate there to meditate for hours and hours, to stop the reasoning mind and to transcend. However, for us to go to India and try to transcend is difficult. In the West, we have a sense of urgency to understand everything, which the Indians lack. As a result, our way is faster than India. It is easier to adapt the knowledge of the Toltecs (or other systems of native Western knowledge) and learn to transform here than it is in India.

The feeling of having been to Teotihuacán before as an Indian Hindu stayed with Miguel and so did his identification with Smoky Mirror. Both visions confirmed that Teotihuacán is a spiritual place, the place where his dream came true.

Before they climbed down from the Pyramid of the Sun, Miguel turned to Gaya and said, "I will be bringing a lot of people here." At that moment, Miguel accepted the responsibility to carry out what don Leonardo had suggested years before when he said that Miguel would spread the knowledge far and wide.

Acting on faith, Miguel organized his first group tour of the site in May 1988, only two months after his visit there with Gaya. He subsequently guided over 60 tours to Teotihuacán. These visits strengthened the process he has re-created spontaneously from his vision about the majestic original purpose of Teotihuacán.

The site at Teotihuacán is a large and mysterious place which has been the centerpiece for many years of exploration and speculation. It lies in Mexico's Central Highlands, 35 miles northeast of Mexico City. The complex of pyramids and temples is laid out along a perfectly straight, wide walkway called the Avenue of the Dead.

Archaeologists agree on a calendar of successive occupations of Teotihuacán, stretching from around 1500 B.C. to 750 A.D. when the area was mysteriously abandoned. From 200 to 600 A.D., during the Tzacualli, Tlamimilolpa, Xolalpan, and Metepec phases, defined in the history of Mexican art as the Classic period, Teotihuacán was the most influential city in all of Mexico. Priests and spiritual warriors, both male and female, were the only residents of the city. A large population lived in surrounding compounds and towns beyond the boundaries of the sacred space that formed the complex. Seven small villages on the outskirts of the site today are living reminders of this once thriving urban center. Today it is known for its pyramids, temples, murals, clay objects, and a few religiously significant stone sculptures.

Ignacio Bernal, on page eight of *Great Sculpture in Ancient Mexico*, explains, "There are few civilizations in which religion has influenced art so thoroughly as in that of ancient Mexico. Although religion is always important as a source of aesthetic inspiration, in this case it had an unusually stimulating effect on the collective imagination, providing innumerable esoteric meanings which were not only translated into art but embodied in the most ordinary objects of everyday life, transforming the real world through symbolic connections which had no counterpart in reality."

Bernal directed the restoration of Teotihuacán from 1962 until 1964, and he was the director of the Museo Nacional de Antropologia in Mexico City for nearly thirty years. He speaks of Teotihuacán as "the Classic city *par excellence*, and possibly the largest capital in ancient America," and he says that Teotihuacán "retains an air of severity" and it was "deeply rooted in its air of imperial security, its preoccupation with rigorous planning. . ." (page 20).

The study of archaeology is mainly concerned with reconstructing the layers of civilizations in a given site through the changes in styles of artifacts. Archaeologists seek explanations about why and when a given people moved to a place and how they lived. They infer beliefs and customs of the various residents from materials found in the area.

While visiting Teotihuacán one might well be interested in the objects found on the site, but it is even more probable that the place arouses a curiosity about its meaning. Controversial but consistently intriguing author Zecharia Sitchin believes the shrines of Teotihuacán may have been built by "gods" who visited the earth from space. He has theorized that these gods landed first in the Middle East. Later the gods directed the Olmecs, who had African features, and another race from the Middle East with Semitic beards and profiles, to begin building Teotihuacán. Their first structures were made bigger and handsomer by later groups of people whose intentions differed from the Olmecs.

In his series of books titled *The Earth Chronicles*, Sitchin theorizes that explorers from the planet Niburu came to earth to search for gold. In their laboratory, they created the first human beings from their own genes blended with that of primitive protohumans. The crossbreeds, who were designed to serve as slaves in the gold mines, at first revered the "gods" who created them. Over time, however, these created slaves developed the intelligence to challenge their creators. They were fertile and populated the planet with a more advanced form of humanity. Our present cycle of evolutionary history begins with them.

In Sitchin's theory, Teotihuacán was originally built for the gods to be a mile-long gold refinery. Water and raw ore were directed downward on a ninety-foot slope to the south through an intricate system of channels whose purpose was to extract gold. The gold was not used at Teotihuacán; instead it was shipped back to Niburu via an intersolar supply system.

Fascinating as such exotic speculation might be, there is another interpretation of Teotihuacán. This is the one that Miguel Angel Ruiz has synthesized from his Toltec ancestry, his repeated visits to Teotihuacán, and his visions while in trance.

Hell on Earth

Fundamental to Miguel's teaching is the concept that earthly life is hell. Hell is the combined dream that all humans share. Both individual and collective dreams are actually nightmares. Every individual has a dream of reality, and likewise, so does each family, each community, city, state, nation, and the whole of humanity. We all contribute to the dream that is characterized by fear.

An ultimate healing would mean to waken from the dream and to thereby be liberated from hell. Teotihuacán was designed for this purpose, to free humans from their fears. Such freedom restores the knowledge that humans are of a divine nature. They are gods. This is the source of the name—Teotihuacán, which means, literally, "the Place Where Men Become Gods."

Through visions, Miguel understands that the people who first settled in the Valley of Teotihuacán came from the Place of the Swans, or Aztlan, somewhere within the Northern United States or possibly Canada. These people were indigenous to the Western Hemisphere, neither nomads from Asia nor refugees from Africa.

When the Aztlans entered the valley, they found a number of caves in which they developed a system of interconnecting tunnels. One of the caves, known as "the Heart of the Universe," became a ceremonial shrine dedicated to the Mother Earth. The cave, a four-part structure in cloverleaf form, has recently been located under the Pyramid of the Sun. The pyramid was deliberately built on top of it. Author John B. Carlson (in "Rise and Fall of the City of the Gods" in *Archaeology*, November–December 1993, pages 58–69) claims that this was a dry four-chambered lava tube. Miguel senses that within the cave at one time there was a lake fed by a river.

In this cave, a man who personified the Smoky Mirror had a dream of being swallowed by a two-headed snake. Smoky Mirror dreamed he was being digested in the body of the snake until all that was left was his essence . . . a beam of light and love. From that original dream, he conceived the entire layout of Teotihuacán as a manifestation of the snake.

By attuning to Smoky Mirror's plan, the properly prepared pilgrim can be led through this site to his own divinity. He can become eternally free from fear. The original purpose of Teotihuacán was to change the dream of all those who survived an initiation into freedom through a ceremonial process.

When Miguel entered into Smoky Mirror's advanced consciousness through his dream, he gained the power to interpret Teotihuacán and to revitalize the ceremonial spiritual passage once conducted there by the original priesthood. Miguel's intention is the same as Smoky Mirror's: to share the knowledge of how a spiritual warrior can follow the Avenue of the Dead from hell to freedom.

The time of Smoky Mirror was long before the eventual decadence that overtook Teotihuacán. In the later period, there were human sacrifices, and hallucinogens were used to reach higher states of awareness, but in the early time of purity that Miguel has tapped into with his vision, neither of these rites were practiced.

On his first visit to Teotihuacán, still affected by overlapping visions, Miguel made his way to the Pyramid of the Moon where Smoky Mirror's spirit is manifested. In the Plaza of the Moon, he felt Smoky Mirror's energies and identified himself with that place where the soul finally exits from the snake's second head in a state of transformation.

The visions Miguel had in 1988 marked the end of his first cycle of work as a nagual healer and teacher. They provoked a new level of synthesis in his shamanic understanding. He had absorbed elements of the nagual tradition from don Leonardo and he had learned about unconditional love from Sarita, but he had gained a profound knowledge of ancient belief systems while in trance states. Later, he had identified completely with Smoky Mirror's dream. Yet, Miguel's own vision is separate from any of those he has been taught or has envisioned. He has transformed everything he has received. The worldview he teaches is a form of magical physics.

CHAPTER THREE

SILENT KNOWLEDGE AND ELEMENTS OF TOLTEC WISDOM

To grasp the brilliance of present-day advanced scientific knowledge requires extensive study. This was also true in prehistoric times when intellectual leaders passed on their scientific knowledge to selected students. Miguel's teachings are a merging of his intuition and his education, including an awareness of astronomy, physics, and biology. His wisdom applies on a shamanic level, a different dimension of reality from the one most scientists study in their laboratories. He offers an effective explanation of the natural world at that place where metaphysical concepts intersect with materiality.

Miguel's students enter a spiral path when they commit themselves to learning what he knows. He repeats the same primal concepts again and again, slowly adding increments of new material. With each repetition, in slightly altered words, his ideas echo in their minds, as he builds a new structure for their world view.

This book follows that spiral path in which Miguel's teaching gradually widens to encompass related ideas grouped around core thoughts. At the originating point of the spiral is a key idea that is known to native people of wisdom throughout the world far back in time: *the universe is a living, highly intelligent being*. Miguel also teaches that the sun is a living being.

Miguel Ruiz:

Every planet is an organ in the solar being. Together, the sun and all the planets are one being. Each unit from an electron to a galaxy is a single being united into larger beings. Our universe is a being made up of the whole system of smaller beings. There are many universes and together they constitute a gigantic being.

In any of the atoms of the body, the electron is like a planet. Living beings on the third electron looking out from their home would view a human body as stars in the same way that people looking out from the earth see stars. As above, so below. The macrocosm is reflected in the microcosm. The same chemical and physical laws affect both the human body and the planets.

As inhabitants of our solar system, we acknowledge the primacy of the sun as our center. Though it is a minor star in the galaxy, the sun is our major star. It provides the light whose energy sustains life on the earth.

All along the life chain, living organisms ingest light. Living creatures take in energy from food and oxygen. The light eaten by humans has already been transformed into food by plants and animals. The human brain transforms this energy from matter into ethereal energy.

How does this happen? In the process of perception we always have an emotional element. The brain creates the emotion and the emotion is a state of energy. Emotion is no longer matter. It is a form of energy.

Material energy is that which is detectable and provable by scientific methods. Ethereal energy cannot be proved within the limits of mainstream science. We cannot prove that hate or love exists, but we experience their effect. Emotional energy is ethereal energy.

For several hundred years, scientists in Europe postulated that the basis of matter in space is an energy known as ether. Miguel says that ether actually exists and the theory of ether is beginning to make its way back into the consciousness of nonmainstream scientists.

Efforts to build so-called Space Power Generators which make use of free energy—ether—in working motors are being funded in a number of countries. (See "Around the Free Energy World in Thirty Days," by Toby Grotz, in *New Science News*, Vol. III, No. 2, page 2.)

Shamans have never doubted that space between the stars, planets, moons, asteroids, galaxies, and universes (and within the atoms of our own bodies) is filled with ether. Ether is the medium of transportation through which information moves.

A basic myth encircles the world in which the following elements are all present:

Miguel Ruiz:

Father Sun brings light and heat to Mother Earth. Mother Earth creates life, the human body, and the mind.

Just as the sperm carries to the womb all the information necessary to create a human being, so the sunlight brings into the earth the energy and the information needed for earth to create life.

This myth is honored by native people everywhere and it is the reason that God is so often represented by the sun. Examples are Apollo and Ra. Mother Earth is the womb.

The sun receives information from the center of the galaxy. Light comes from other stars as well as the sun. The universe communicates with itself through light. Condensed light is a nerve found throughout the universe. Throughout the universe there is a constant flow of information. Data moves in beams of light from the sun and other stars. Light beams are therefore messengers, and one synonym for messenger is "angel." A light ray is an angel. An angel is a being of light carrying information outward from the center of our galaxy, star to star, sun to planet.

Our seemingly solid bodies are created from condensed sunlight, making us vessels of light, just like angels. Our true identity is angelic, or light-filled. We are beings filled with the information that comes to earth in light.

The primary source of all information is at the center of the universe. In our region of the universe, the source is at the center of the Milky Way, our own galaxy. Locally, our source is the sun. (There are numerous universes besides the one we inhabit.)

The information carried by light is known as *the silent knowledge*. The secret of this wisdom is the coded method of continually renewing life. This life-preserving data in our sunlight is decoded by Planet Earth.

Miguel Ruiz:

The earth is both an organ in the body of the solar being and a complete system, or living body, in itself. The earth transforms the energy of light into ever-renewed earthly life. Within living cells, the silent knowledge is stored and passed on in DNA; therefore our own bodies are storehouses of this wisdom.

Earth has its own metabolism and it also has organs. The sun's energy is processed by the organs of the earth and then is released back to the sun, like an inhalation and an exhalation of breath. Among the earth's "organs" are its atmosphere, which functions like the skin of the planet, the oceans, the forests, and all animals. The totality of human beings forms an organ of the earth. The function of the human organ is to transform energy from matter to the ethereal, and conversely to transform ethereal energy into matter.

Native people even now recognize each organ of the earth as a god. There is a god of the ocean, a god of the air, and a god that represents all humans. There are personal gods and family gods, and a god for each nation. Instead of calling them gods today, we speak of "the spirit of the nation," but it is still a god.

Gods are created in the mind of humans. What does god mean? God means an entity superior to a human. It protects the earth to think that there is a god for the air, a god for the sea, and to venerate that godlike energy. One can imagine the positive result if the majority of humans praised each of the earth's organs, including the whole of humanity. In addition to the gods who represent earth's organs, humans have revered other gods who came from elsewhere in the universe.

We are now at a momentous point in the history of life on earth. Some celestial programming is underway. All hidden ancient traditions are being opened at once. The opening of the silent knowledge is a response to a signal from the intelligence at the center of our galaxy, the Milky Way, via our sun.

Miguel states that we entered the Sixth Sun on January 11, 1992, just as it was predicted in the Aztec calendar. Energy from the sun abruptly altered on that day. Miguel was in Teotihuacán for the anticipated event with a group of his students. He saw the color of the light change. The vibration of our sunlight became faster and gentler. Miguel channeled the new light and performed a ceremony to receive the birth of the Sixth Sun. He describes what happened there as a miracle. His companions noticed a change in him and then felt it in themselves as they stood within the complex of temples where the new sunlight was received with a special charge. All life on the planet and the planet itself are affected by the change in DNA.

Miguel Ruiz:

DNA (deoxyribonucleic acid, the basic substance, which takes the form of a double helix, found in the nucleus of every cell, which is associated with the transmission of genetic information) is a specific vibration of light that comes from the sun and becomes matter. Every kind of life on Planet Earth, from the stones to humans, has a specific vibration from light that comes from the sun. Each plant, animal, virus, and bacterium has a specific ray of light. It is condensed by Mother Earth and the information carried in the light becomes matter. This reproduction is the method whereby the silent knowledge is passed down from generation to generation of different life. DNA is specific to every form of life. Science has not yet differentiated the subtle distinctions in forms of DNA.

We have come to the beginning of a new dispensation. It could mean a relaxation of the harmful attitudes we have been harboring, but there is an implicit sense that we might not change as fast as necessary to avert predicted natural disasters. Changes in the earth's axis, in climate, and in the crust of the earth are possible because earth is experiencing the new energy as an opportunity to heal itself.

The change in vibratory energy coming into the earth has not gone unnoticed among certain scientists. Ron Radhoff writes, "in 1962, the year many say we entered into the Aquarian Age, we began to enter into the influence of (the) photon-belt encircling the Pleiades. We will pass into the center of it by the year 2011. . . . St. Germain . . . refers to the photon-belt as the Golden Nebula, a parallel universe of much higher vibration. Little by little it is absorbing our universe. As we merge with this higher vibration universe, it will become the catalyst for massive changes." (*New Science News*, Vol. III, No. 2, page 7)

During the years of the Fifth Sun, incoming solar energy had a harsh effect on human beings and, through us, on the earth. The purpose of the present change in energy is to alter the dream that humanity is projecting onto itself and the earth. We will move from a nightmare of hell to a dream of heaven on earth. Heaven is a place without fear.

Elements of Toltec Wisdom

The Toltec tradition forms a chain. Miguel learned from his grand-father, Leonardo Macias, and he learned from his father. Father to son. Miguel can trace his family to the early 1700s, but he does not know where the chain began. He says, "I come from the Toltecs, people who lived thousands of years ago and are still alive. Toltec means 'men of knowledge'. . . that's what all of us are."

The Toltec tradition is a way of life, not just a way of knowledge. The goal of this way is happiness. To achieve happiness, you need to express who you really are, not the person other people expect you to be. Through a process of self-scrutiny, you can discover who you were before you were domesticated. Then you can recover the freedom to use your own mind, your own body, your own brain to express yourself outside the dream which is life. To achieve that freedom, the Toltecs developed three masteries.

I. **Mastery of Awareness.** Through this mastery, one becomes aware that humans are dreaming all the time, day and night. They are creating the dream of hell. The way out of the nightmare is to know where you are, what you are, and what kind of freedom you seek.

II. **Mastery of Transformation**. This is also known as Mastery of Stalk-ing. Through this mastery one gains control over one's emotions.

Miguel Ruiz:

Once we have the awareness that in our minds we are the slaves of the Judge and the Victim who dictate our emotions, we can, through the Mastery of Transformation, challenge our whole belief system. Our goal is to recover who we really are, to be ourselves, and to allow our spirit to express itself into the outside dream. By choosing our actions and reactions in everything that we do, the Master of Transformation becomes a master of freedom, a master of surrendering, and a master of love.

III. **Mastery of Intent**. This is the mastery of the spirit and the will. The Master of Intent becomes One with God. God works through the master's mouth, mind, and hands. In that state, with every action the master does, there is God.

The Toltecs' goal is have communion with the Creator, the Spirit. They seek to go back home. In their teaching, they say we came from the Creator and we will return to the Creator. Miguel speaks of the Creator as Father, and he uses the masculine pronoun.

Eknath Easwaran, in his book *Meditation*, explains his use of the word Lord in a way that is in empathy with Miguel's. "When I use words like 'Lord' or 'God,' I mean the very ground of existence, the most profound thing we can conceive of. This supreme reality is not something outside us, something separate from us. It is within, at the core of our being—our real nature, nearer to us than our bodies, dearer to us than our lives." (page 30)

The Toltec tradition is a map that tells you how to go home. Because it is a map, you have to begin at the point where you are. Your first task is to become aware of what you really are, and this is a mystery.

Miguel Ruiz:

To explain what you are, you could just say your name. Or, you could say, "I was born and I'm going to die." You are a human, a man or a woman. You are a doctor, a lawyer, a teacher, whatever you do. You are your body. You think that you are what you feel. But is all of that true? Is that what you really are?

We ask eternal questions. What is God? What is the universe? What is death? What is the Planet Earth? What is matter? What is light? Science tries to explain material questions. There is an amazing amount of knowledge available to us, but behind that knowledge is the mystery. What is behind electrons? What is behind galaxies? What is behind the spirit? Did we exist before we were born? What happens when we die? We say, "I am," but what does it really mean?

As a medical doctor, I could say "I am a human body, a perfect biological machine with a marvelous brain that has been made by billions of little computers that are the neurons. It is made by little living beings that are the cells that make organs and muscles. I am that complex which is human."

What makes that possible? What is the human brain? How does the brain work? We have tried so hard to explain it by microscope and electronics. We have had amazing results from our experiments, yet we still do not know what the brain is.

You are going to die, but now you are alive. What is life? It is useless for us to reason in order to understand something that is impossible to understand. Our reason tells us what is truth and what is not. Reason makes the decision, this is what I am and this is what I am not. However, these decisions are merely limits, not possibilities.

If I say I am happy, you can understand me. You have a concept of happiness. When I feel pain, either physical or emotional pain, I have to use words and concepts to describe it, yet they do not explain it. Anger and jealousy are nothing but concepts. The truth is we are a great mystery.

Because I have the Mastery of Transformation, I am aware that everything, including myself, is energy in motion.

Miguel refers to an object that seems to be solid, yet we can prove scientifically that it is composed of atoms. Atoms are constantly moving. Although the object seems solid, it is actually moving energy. The space between atoms is larger than the mass of the atoms themselves. We perceive things as stable, but everything is in constant motion.

Miguel Ruiz:

What we see is nothing but the light reflecting from objects. Reflected light gives them apparent form. We have agreed to accept our visual perception of reality as the truth, but this truth derives from an arrangement or consensus in which we are a partner. Perception is a miracle that demonstrates our power to create the outside reality. We perceive the natural world, but we actually created it in our mind and brain.

We have created language, and we use it to name all the animals and plants and other components of this universe. Naming things seems to authenticate the world of illusion. The reality we have made gives us a false sense of security.

We feel we have our feet on the ground. We see the sky. We sense the wind and the rain. It is familiar to us. It is all a dream made by the mind. It is a dream with matter and structure because we made it that way with our own magic. All of us are magicians.

Because we have the power to create this reality, we are related to everything in this reality. What I see with my eyes and hear with my ears is true only in this reality. If I shift my point of view a little, it is not truth anymore.

We are all traveling together on the spaceship of Planet Earth. We are moving through space at tremendous velocity. Because we are all moving at the same speed, we feel as though nothing has moved. If we could stop just for a moment while the rest of the world moves, we would see a different reality.

When we shift our point of view, we see that our body is matter which is energy that allows us to move. Another kind of energy is all around us that is also us, and this is the mind. The mind is energy but it is not matter. We think. We feel. We dream. But we cannot take a piece of a dream into the laboratory and prove that it exists. We cannot take love into the laboratory and say, "This is love." We do not prove that an emotion exists, but we know that love exists because we can feel it. It is not matter, but it is energy. It is energy because it exists. Everything that exists is energy. Energy cannot be destroyed. It can only be transformed. Energy has no beginning and no end.

This sounds familiar. When we go to church, we hear such words said about God. God and energy are exactly the same. Everything is made by energy and everything is made by God. There are billions of manifestations of energy. There are billions of manifestations of God because everything is God.

The mind is energy that is not matter. The mind is ethereal energy. All energy is alive, so the mind is alive. Not only is the body alive, but the mind is also and we are the mind as well as the body. We mix the material and the ethereal energy in the concept "I am."

At the same time that we are talking, our mind is actively thinking. It is dreaming. Our eyes perceive the light, but the mind makes an interpretation of that light and creates this reality. It is possible to reach a point at which the separation of mind and body dissolves and reality itself will change completely.

Individuality is a false concept. We are not individuals. We are just a little piece of the chain that is life. Your human body is made by billions of cells. Every little cell is a living being that can exist outside of your body. It can even reproduce outside of your body. You are that cell also. The cell itself has many inner elements and each of them is alive. The cell is part of a chain. With billions of cells we make a human body. You can say, "I am the body." Meanwhile, each cell can say, "I am a cell." The cell lacks awareness that many cells together make an organ. The liver, the heart, the intestines, the brain, the eyes—all the organs together form a human body, which is a unity.

Each of us is a human being. Yet, just like a cell, we think we are separate and we are not. All humans on the planet create another organ for a larger living being, which is the earth. Planet Earth is a living being. We are the Planet Earth. A single cell is human. A single person is the planet. All humans form only one of earth's organs. There are many others. The trees, the atmosphere, the ocean, rocks, and animals are all organs of the earth.

The earth has etheric energy just like humans do. It has a soul. It has a mind. It is alive. It is a living being. It has a metabolism through which it receives energy from the outside. It transforms energy that it takes in and sends out its own form of energy.

Planets receive energy from the sun and transform it. On earth, animals eat plants and transform the energy they receive. Humans eat plants and animals and transform the energy they receive from them.

What is the function of the organ in earth's body that humanity constitutes? It is to transform material energy into ethereal energy. We receive food and oxygen, and with our brains we transform the energy of matter into ethereal energy.

We work for the earth twenty-four hours a day, just like the bees and the ants. The work we do for the planet is to make emotions. Making emotions is the main function of the human mind.

We are dreaming when we are awake and when we are asleep. When you sleep and dream, your dream creates emotions. When you are awake and dream, the dream has a structure. Even though we are dreaming, we are interpreting everything we experience. To do so, we impel our brain to create emotions. This is our function.

Planet Earth is one element in a chain. The whole universe is alive. It is a living being. This planet is just a little piece of the living being that is the universe.

Who we are is now somewhat expanded. We are the body. We are the mind. We are also Planet Earth. There is information in the large chain that is the universe. The same information is in the earth. Likewise, all the information in one human body is in one cell of the body.

One cell has all the information needed and all the power to create its own universe in the form of another human being. One human being has all the power and information it needs to create another planet. Such an act of creation does not depend upon reason. This creation from within depends upon the silent knowledge.

Even the cell is as powerful as the human body, and the human body is as powerful as the earth, and the earth is as powerful as the whole universe.

At each step in this chain, it is necessary to change one's point of view to perceive the analogue. From the microcosm to the macrocosm, one system is operating. It is all a mystery. From outside the human point of view, it is possible to see the complexity of the human being and to see the relationship of the human to the total mystery of the universe. Wherever we go, we are there waiting for ourselves.

Each human being compares with a cell in a muscle. We are the same interchangeable cells. If I am you and you are me, I have no reason to hurt you. If you are me, why do you have to hurt me? If I am my planet, why do I have to destroy the planet? Why don't I understand the planet? Why don't I understand you?

We might recognize ourselves by our names, our personalites, our separateness, but when we alter our point of view, the concept of individuality seems very limited. We are not individuals. We are One. That One is ultimately all universes together. This is the big mystery. This is God.

God is only a concept. It is a title, like a lawyer or a doctor. The concept of God is too small for the reality of what God is, but it is an explanation that our reason accepts. We lack adequate words to explain God, but the word God is understandable to us. In reality, God is life. Life is action. We are God and God is us.

As part of the human organ of the planet, we are connected with every other part of the planet. Whatever happens to the planet affects everyone within the human organ; and vice versa, whatever affects a single person within the human organ, affects the entire planet. Like a single cell that has the power to create a human being, deep inside of us we have the power to create a whole universe.

Our reasoning is so limited that it prevents us from understanding the scope of our power. We have the power to change everything. We can transform. We can build or destroy. Our power is greater than any atomic bomb. Our power is our intent, our spirit. This is our silent knowledge.

Reason does not know that we know. Reason is only a small part of the mind. Reason does not make decisions. It has one function and that is to connect two different dreams, the dream of the planet with the individual dream.

The mind is made by emotions. Emotions are the code that builds the mind. Just as numbers are the code for mathematics, and notes are the code for music, emotions are the code for the whole mind. Every emotion is alive and is a living being. Just as every cell in our body is alive and creates the human body, so every emotion is alive. The mind is also alive and is a living being. Mind connects all human beings. All human minds together form the largest part of the mind of the planet itself.

The strongest scientific point of view today is still focused on earth as an object. When a volcano erupts or a hurricane howls, science offers a technical explanation for the event. In Toltec wisdom, the earth has decided to take these actions. The planet is a living being who can think and make decisions for itself.

Toltec ancestors understood that earth is a living being. Such a worldview is still held by native peoples all around the world. If the ground is parched, they dance to bring rain. They play the drum and sing. They build a fire. The important part of their ritual is that they make their intent to Mother Earth to bring them water and earth responds. They do not consider the relationship of their intent and the earth's reaction to be a mystery. This level of relationship cannot be understood through the reason alone. The native point of view is that of a shaman. In order to transform, humans will need to recover the shamanic perspective.

We cannot see an electron with our human eye because our eye is not designed to see it. Our eye operates within a certain time and space. The electron's time and space of operation are completely different from the eye's. To see an electron, we would need to be another electron in an identical time and space. Because we are filled with electrons, we can grasp the concept of electrons. We have emotions, so we can understand emotions. We do not perceive them with our eyes. This kind of perception is closer to the intuitive and shamanic than it is to the analytical process of our reason. We are connected with everything and we affect everything through our intent. Our intent is a different part of our mind than our reason.

One human being within the earth's organ of humanity compares to a neuron within the human body. One neuron can make a decision and the whole body will obey. Likewise, one human can make a decision and the elements will obey. The elements are obedient to human intent.

To bring on the rain, you must transform your point of view and become one with the rain and the atmosphere. When you are in harmony with their vibration, anything can happen. You can apply this same principle to identifying with an animal, or any other organ of the planet. We can extend this process to include the entire universe, not just the earth.

When the relationship of the human to the whole universe is understood, it is easy to see that there is truth in astrology. Astrology is a science rather than a tool of divination. Ancient Toltecs knew that the universe is a living being that has a metabolism. Astrology was a study of the metabolism of the universe.

The Toltecs were seers who knew what would happen to the planet because they could interpret the quality of energy the universe needed from the earth.

We create emotional energy and this is the main form of energy that the earth transmits to the sun. From the sun, emotional energy is radiated outward to the rest of the universe. The sun controls the earth and it makes decisions that affect the earth.

The sun sends us light. In sunlight is all the information the sun intends to send to earth. Light is energy. All energy has memory, so all information can be stored in light. Sunlight carries information for the whole planet. It causes reactions in the earth. The earth contains ethereal, material and emotional energy. In reaction to the information coded in sunlight, the earth will respond by sending the energy intended by the sun.

Teilhard de Chardin, the great Jesuit philosopher, gave the name "noosphere" to the quality of mind and thought which encircles the globe. The noosphere is the mind organ which is made of all human minds together. Such an idea explains the simultaneity of inventions and the manner in which an idea moves swiftly from mind to mind and leads to changes in human thought.

Rupert Sheldrake is a British biochemist who proposed the theory of formative causation, in which each natural system, from crystals to humans, shares a morphic field. The individual entities within each field inherit a collective memory. Their memory directs their habits of behavior and reproduction according to their kind. Within a specific field, a "morphic resonance" operates across space and time. Each field is a whole and all fields are in constant evolution, from atoms to galaxies. Over time, systems have died out and disappeared.

Sheldrake writes, "According to the hypothesis of formative causation, these fields in some sense still exist, although they cannot be expressed because there is nothing to tune in to them. Even the fields of dinosaurs are potentially present here and now; but there are no appropriate tuning systems, such as living dinosaur eggs, that can pick them up by morphic resonance.

"If for any reason—for example a genetic mutation or an unusual environmental stress—any living system comes into resonance with the fields of an ancestral or extinct type, then these fields could be expressed again, and archaic structures could suddenly reappear. . . ." (*The Presence of the Past,* pages 285–286)

Sheldrake's hypothesis is in keeping with Miguel's Toltec visions in several ways. Miguel himself must be a living system who is in resonance with the ancient Toltecs, because their dream has come alive in him and he is developing a field of others who will share the dream.

Miguel's explanation of the relationship of the sun, the earth, and human life is similar to Sheldrake's concepts. Miguel directs us to the sun as the center of all information and intelligence in the solar system. Although the sun is also a recipient of information from an even larger living system in the center of the galaxy, for us living on earth, the sun is the source of our evolution.

Miguel describes a continuous river of light moving from the sun to the earth that contains the vibrations of each individual and each field of life on earth. The light from the sun is the cause of effects within an individual, or within the entire field of related living beings. For an evolutionary change to occur, the sun emits an altered vibration of sunlight. The receptive organism responds and transmits its response back to the sun in a constant interaction of energies.

A nagual such as Miguel can "see" this river of light. This is how he could see the light change in January of 1992 during his visit to Teotihuacán.

Miguel Ruiz:

At the moment of the change in the light, we began metabolizing a different quality of energy. It is difficult to test in a laboratory because, through science, we do not understand light as a living being.

Our eyes "eat" this new light in the form of food, which is now of a higher quality. It will affect our minds, not our genes.

It is basically undetectable by our limited science now, but in time we will prove that light is a living biological being with intelligence, and the source of our own intelligence.

Each human has some frequency of light, which is always existent in the sun. This frequency is always connected like a river to earth. This river is permanent, as long as the sun and the earth exist. If we shift our point of view in terms of time and space, it is possible to see that river of light as something solid in the same way that, in our time and space, we see a human hand as something solid. We already know that, if we shift our point of view to a smaller, swifter time and space, we no longer see the human hand as solid. Instead, we can see all the atoms, all the electrons as a field of energy that is moving and is not solid. The river of light, like any river, keeps its form but it is never the same.

A ray of light has perception and awareness. Billions of light rays connect the sun and the earth. From this light, humans are brought to life and they "eat" this light in a continuous process of action and reaction.

Information within the body changes the cells in the brain and elsewhere. A single human changes the way he metabolizes sunlight in reaction to the sun and transmits his or her response back to the sun.

The sun processes the change.

The whole river of light has a new quality. It then affects the whole of humanity because this particular quality of light reaches all humans.

Such a system of action and reaction explains the efficacy of prayer. The prayerful intent of human beings goes back to the sun in the river of light.

The nagual is the human who develops a small replica of the sun within his will. We call this the black sun because it is light that cannot be perceived by the human eye.

The nagual perceives the river of light that connects with all life on the planet. It is a huge river. The nagual can see even in the light river all the separate rays, a separate ray for each person. Other naguals have witnessed the line of consciousness, the ray of light, as humans modify their own consciousness.

The light is now intensifying human creativity, imagination, and intelligence.

We find a similarity between the process of change in the whole of humanity (the human organ of earth) and the normal hormonal process of a girl becoming a woman. There is a whole universe within the girl's body, including her organs, blood, nerves, digestive system, brain, and all communicative systems that operate between systems.

The sun and the earth are part of one living system. We can say that when the earth is mature enough, it sends a message to the sun. The sun reacts and sends its message to trigger an evolutionary change in humanity. The sun acts as the brain, just as the woman's brain initiates the hormonal change in her body that brings her to maturity.

Humans lack the means to transcribe the exact code in which information comes from the stars, but parts of the mind and soul can understand it. We can channel this information. Earth, as a living being, easily understands the messages it receives.

The earth emits light, but not at a frequency seen by the human eye. In response to receiving messages in sunlight, the earth replies by transmitting its own light. This light can be etheric or emotional light.

There are many extraterrestrials on earth. Most of them are nothing but light. Once they have arrived on the planet they can take different forms. The easiest way to travel in space is not on a spaceship, but through light. Toltecs used to do that and so did the Egyptians.

They traveled from one planet to another via the light. We all have the power to do this. The Mastery of Awareness from the Toltecs will remind us that we have this power.

I am not teaching anything. I am just reminding others of what they have remembered that they know. The knowledge I bear is not my own. It is in everyone.

Around the world, all cultures have the same knowledge. All human beings have the same information inside. It might be phrased with different words, but the knowledge is exactly the same. The Mastery of Awareness is so extensive that it demands commitment of time and practice to remember the silent knowledge we each have within us. The call is to recollect all of the knowledge and to be what we really are so that we can use our inner power. We aspire to become One with God.

In the second Mastery of Transformation, we learn to be the stalker. This is how to recover what we are. In this mastery, we learn to clean the mind, to stop suffering, to become warriors, to become masters, to become free, to become one with love.

The third Mastery of Intent is the result when we are no longer the body and no longer the mind. We are no longer the soul. We are just love, because love includes everything. Love is the real name of God. Love is everywhere. Everything is made of love.

Love has billions of expressions, including fear. Fear is a reflection of love, but it is only a small part of love's expressions. Fear will control the mind. The mind will control the brain. What you do is according to what you perceive, so if you are feeling fear, what you perceive will be analyzed with fear. We see in the eyes the expression of what a person has in his or her mind. You will perceive the outside dream according to your eyes. If you have eyes of sadness, you will feel sad whether it is raining or sunny. If you have eyes of love, you will see love wherever you go.

Trees are made by love. Animals are made by love. The water we drink and the rivers and oceans are made by love. If you perceive love, you will connect with anything else that is made by love. You can become the eagle. You can become the wind, or the rain, or the clouds. All becomes One. You will recognize that everything is perfect just as it is.

Our path to the silent knowledge is through awareness. We go deep into hell and we suffer in order to acquire awareness. This is why we decided to take a human form and to have a human mind which dreams this kind of dream, the nightmare we call hell.

To get from hell, we need awareness which we acquire through intent and spirit. We become Godlike because we have awareness, not just because we have silent knowledge. Knowledge alone is not sufficient. We must express our knowledge in action.

There are many ways to become aware. In India the path is through devotion and effort. In Christianity, it is through guilt, until we discover we have no reason to be guilty at all. Guilt is a manmade emotion to make ourselves suffer for something we really want to do. How ridiculous it is to suffer for something we want.

My way is in nagualism. On this path, everyone has a chance to become aware because nagualism avoids judgment. The way to freedom through nagualism is to stop judging and to stop victimization. The way is open to everyone. We do not need to be special. Even the person who is addicted to drugs or alcohol can make it on this path. Sometimes it is fast and other times it is slow, but it is available to all. This map of how to get out of hell, how to transform from being a victim to being a free warrior, does not place the end goal in the afterlife.

In nagualism, you can bring heaven to earth. You can live in heaven while your body is alive. You can do it because I did it. If I can do it, you can do it. Jesus told us the same thing.

Information that is essential to our escape from the dream of the planet is vital to the expansion of science as well. When science accepts the notion that earth is alive, scientific theory will expand and grow. With the further idea that the universe is alive and all of us are fundamentally connected, science again can move forward. All our minds become One. This concept will alter psychology. Other basic ideas from the Toltecs—such as that the mind is made by emotions, that we are dreaming twenty-four hours a day, that we have a Judge and a Victim within us as a result of our domestication (and we are domesticated animals), that the mind is alive, that every emotion is a living being able to live inside and outside our mind, that we create emotions and send them to others telepathically—are the ingredients for a far more expansive philosophical basis for life.

One mind-boggling Toltec concept is that we can transfer our consciousness from our reason to our will. This shift is the source of our potential power to completely transform the planet and to become God. We can control ethereal energy. We can control our own dream and have a beneficial effect on everyone else's dream. Each of these thoughts can have far-ranging consequences in the mind of humans. From acceptance of Toltec silent knowledge, the individual has access to a form of magic that is innately human, but this magic is rarely presented through orthodox channels.

Exercise:

Please record on tape in your own voice the following exercise. Then close your eyes and listen. Use your imagination to dream this story.

Miguel Ruiz:

In this dream I find myself in the most beautiful forest at midday. I am completely comfortable surrounded by beauty. I see the sunbeams lighting the trees and the flowers. I see butterflies and I hear the sound of the river. I walk to that river where an old man sits beneath a big tree. With his white beard and strong, kind eyes, the man emits a radiant aura of beautiful colors. I sit in front of him and wait until he feels my presence and looks at me.

I ask, "How can you send out these beautiful colors and can you teach me how to do it?"

He smiles at me. "Your request brings back memories for me because one day I saw my own teacher doing the same thing and I asked him the same question. As an answer, he opened his chest and he reached in and pulled out his own heart. From within it, he took a radiant flame. He opened my chest and put that flame inside my heart. From that moment on, everything changed inside me because that flame was unconditional love. I felt the flame of that love and it became a consuming fire.

"I shared that love with and gave unconditional love to every cell in my body. That day I became one with my own body.

"I decided to love my mind. I loved every emotion, every thought, every feeling, and every dream. That fire transformed my mind completely and my mind loved me back so much that the fire grew even more and I had the need to share my love even more.

"I decided to put my love in every tree, in every flower, every blade of grass, and all the plants in the whole forest. They reacted to my love and they loved me also and we became one.

"But, still my love grew more and more so I had an even greater need to share my love. I decided to put a little piece of my love in every rock, in the dirt, in every metal on the earth, and they loved me back. We became one.

"My love still grew. I decided to put a little love in every animal that exists, in the birds, the cats, and the dogs. They loved me back and they protected me. We became one.

"My love still grew and I decided to love the water. I loved the rain, the snow, the rivers, the lakes, the oceans, and I became one with the water.

"When my love continued to grow, I decided to love the atmosphere, the breeze, the hurricane, the tornado, and we became one and they loved me back.

"My love did not end there. It grew even more and I turned my face to the sky where I saw the sun, the moon, and the stars. I decided to put a piece of my love in them and they loved me back and we became one.

"Again, my love expanded and I decided to share it with every human, with the elders, with every man, woman, and child, and we became one.

"Now, wherever I go, I am there waiting for myself."

Then that old man opened his chest with his hands and took his heart out before my eyes. He took a flame from his heart and he opened my chest and my heart and he put that flame in my heart. When I awoke and opened my eyes, I felt that flame become a fire. Now I share my love with you.

At this moment, I open my chest and in front of your eyes I open my heart. I take a small flame and I open your chest and your heart. I put that flame in your heart. That flame of my love is the flame of the Christ.

And that is the dream.

CHAPTER FOUR

THE DREAM OF HELL

Hell is a concept that is found in more than one religion. Hell is described as a place of suffering, fear, violence, and injustice, where everybody punishes everybody else. Hell is a human mental state. Other animals have no hell of their own, although they may be victimized by human hellishness. Hell is not in the body or the soul; it is only in the human mind. Hell is the way we humans dream our life.

Miguel Ruiz:

Let's begin our study of "getting out of hell" with a prayer.

Put your attention on your heart. Put your hands on your heart and feel your heartbeat. This is the motor of your body. The heart is a wonderful biological machine that serves you. It's a gift from the Angel of Death to you, from the Angel of Life to you.

You use your body to express what you are. As you feel and perceive the world around you, all the energy becomes one with the universe inside you. Feel that life.

Your body without you is nothing. Without you, your body can collapse at any moment. It is the same with your mind. Without you, your mind cannot dream or think. Without you, your mind has no memory. You are the force that makes it possible for your body to have life.

Your soul, mind, and body are gifts for you. Without you, your body dies. Your mind collapses. Your soul dissolves. All life is ONE and the same.

"We ask you, Lord, to make your manifestation to us so that we can perceive what we really are. We ask you, Lord, to grant us the opportunity to experience what we really are. Let it be for everyone the way it is for me. I know what I really am. Each of us is really a manifestation of love. I am you and you are me. Thank you, Lord. Amen."

I want to review some basic concepts that give us a better understanding of what it means to get out of hell. I like to see hell from outside the dream.

The human mind is a living being, but it is a different kind of being than a body. The body, made from material energy, is a biological machine. The mind is a biological machine that is made from ethereal energy. Ethereal is another name for the energy we experience, but we cannot prove it exists. The body's existence can be proved. We know we have a mind, emotions, reason, and intellect because we perceive them. We have named them.

Our mind is made by our emotions. Everything the mind perceives has an emotional component. When light of varying frequencies strikes material objects, it is reflected into our eye. The brain translates these light images of material energy into matter, and what the mind creates we perceive as reality. Actually, this reality is a dream. We dream twenty-four hours a day, whether our brain is awake or asleep.

The brain can change energy in both directions. It has the capacity to transform material energy to ethereal energy. We create ideas, and ideas are ethereal energy. When the brain converts ideas into words and writing, we make a manifestation in the material world of what is happening in our mind. The mind creates imagination, and the imagination dreams. The way we dream leads us into suffering and emotional pain.

The priest says to his congregation, "If you don't do what the church says, you will go to hell." Well, I have bad news for him. We are already there. We suffer because of our interaction with other humans. In our interactions, we are constantly judging and struggling to understand. Due to the lack of communication that creates chaos among people, our interpretation of human interaction leads to the dream of hell.

Most relationships are marred by the need to control each other. In forming your relationships, you had a choice of thousands of humans. When you choose a person to love, you have to pick someone who is right. You need a partner who accepts you as you are because you will stay as you are. If you want to change another without being changed, look for someone else, otherwise, you are creating your own nightmare. If you accept a job and refuse to train for it, then you have a problem. Fear is all around due to these things.

Each of us has a private dream. Our family shares a dream, too, with its own goals, rules, and conflicts. Every group has a shared dream, from the individual to the nation to the planet. The dream of all humanity is the dream in the mind of Planet Earth. The earth's dream varies from place to place. Each area has its own rules, based on separate dreams that are part of the whole dream. Thus we can see that beyond our private dream is the collective dream of all humans, which we share. Our despair rests on the fact that we don't know we are dreaming. This is the reason we live in the nightmare of hell.

The fears in one human mind become bigger when they are projected outside. Our community is a society of fear, injustice, and punishment. Our teenagers are killing each other, and we find crime and hatred in all parts of the world. Even our entertainment is studded with violence.

Hell is a disease in the human mind. The whole world is a hospital.

Heaven is exactly the opposite of hell. It is a place of joy, love, peace, communication, and understanding, with neither a Judge nor a Victim. In heaven there is clarity. You know what you are. You no longer blame yourself or others.

Miguel reminds his students that all humans dream together. A dream is a living being. We create the dream. The dream creates our life. A culture is a dream of many people together. Every person, family, city, society, and the world has dreams.

Our gods are created in our dreams. Each god has a beginning, a middle, and an end. The god accrues power as it grows. It conquers and rises to the top. Then, people start looking for justice. When they cannot find it, their god decays. We can now witness the decaying years of our gods and the state of injustice that our beliefs have created.

Throughout the two thousand years of the Piscean Age, which is just coming to an end, our dream and our gods have not been in harmony.

All humans are dreaming little dreams which together make up the nightmare of hell that we call reality. We have only to look at the news to see the war, violence, crime, and distrust that prove the nightmarishness of our collective dream.

One of our widely shared dreams is of Jesus, but our dream of him is far from the one that this radiant spirit meant to bring to the world. His effort was to reform the dream of his people with his message of love and compassion. His dream was one of heaven on earth. The Jews of his day were sacrificing animals in the temple and using the temple as a marketplace. Jesus claimed that his father god did not ask for blood. He drove the moneychangers out of the sacred precinct. By his actions and words he threatened the status quo of Jewish and Roman leaders who defended their positions by plotting against him. As a result, Jesus mostly failed in his mission to change the dream of the planet, but his influence played its assigned role in the evolution of the human species.

A portion of Jesus' message was preserved in its original form. Through the centuries, the Christ energy has benefitted generations of the faithful whose ideals have changed the dream of the planet to a certain extent. However, Jesus' dream of love was exploited and corrupted by successive power seekers among his followers, particularly by Constantine who "converted" to Christianity in order to weld its influence to that of the Roman Empire.

Miguel says that the name of Jesus became a demon. As Europe was conquered, the name of Jesus and the Christian message were misused for the sake of power. The true message of the Christ went forth as beams of light that entered into sacred sites around the world, just as the ancient wisdom of native people was driven underground. The reigning powers in the world destroyed the spiritual self-confidence of the people they ruled. Among their destructive ideas are original sin, the separation of humans from each other, from nature, and from God, and the fear of eternal punishment in hell. Institutionalized religious, economic, and political powers have held people in thrall. The Crusades and the Inquisition were instruments of expansion and control to maintain secular and religious power structures. Conquest and coercive religious conversion were also means used for domination. Miseries spread in Jesus' name became the nightmare of the Western Hemisphere, too, and it remains so, although the nightmare is in a weakened condition.

In areas of the world where Jesus does not stand for the demon, another demon takes his place. The nightmare is the dream of almost everyone on earth. Mohammed is demonized by the Muslims who use his name to wreak vengeance on their enemies. Human degradation in Asian countries comes from an indifference toward life based on a misunderstanding of Buddha's dream. In totalitarian countries, suffering for the good of the state is praised. All versions of the nightmare are prompted by fear.

Miguel reveres the pure vibrations of the Buddha and the Christ and many other spiritual souls who have gone before us. His teaching is not meant to be irreverent toward, nor destructive of, deep faith in the pure nature of these avatars who brought the pearl of truth to earth and inserted it into the collective mind of humans. Though the nightmare of hell has triumphed, a memory of life without fear has left its trace in human consciousness.

Miguel's intention is to awaken people to the harmful effects of the distorted fears that encrust the original inspirations of advanced souls like the Christ and Buddha. In their present state of corruption, religions sustain the nightmare of hell.

It is necessary to add here that Miguel does not believe it is beneficial, at this stage in our human evolution, to withdraw religious training from our children. He stresses that a child must learn the full system of thought that leads to our dream of hell before he or she can transform the dream into one of heaven on earth.

Almost every sacred book holds a memory of a human race prior to our own that had an advanced civilization. Their race had some means for aerial flight and a worldwide communication system just as we have today. Miguel teaches that this race was the Third Humanity that lasted for thousands of years in harmony before it destroyed itself through nuclear war and the ensuing radiation.

This early race—and it is only one of many that lived on earth before our time—offers us a warning that our beliefs, like theirs, could lead us to a similar fatal result if we continue to hold onto false ideas that create imbalance, disharmony, and fear.

Our contemporary reverence for science and technology, and our denial of the validity of information available through intuition and revelation, are driving us further from our divine nature and closer to the fate of our predecessors.

In most areas of the world, we have given primacy to a totally masculine image of God. At the same time, we have excluded the feminine aspect of God's nature. Earth, which expresses the feminine principle, has been abused because of our belief that mankind was given dominion over the natural world.

The advanced race that was destroyed has left signs and warnings for us at certain key places on the earth that have been recognized as sacred. The Great Pyramid at Giza is one of these sites. Hermes Trismegistus (the Greek name for the Egyptian god Thoth), from whom the word "hermetic" is derived, is the legendary author of works on alchemy, astrology, and magic. Miguel believes such a man did indeed live in Egypt. Hermes rediscovered ancient knowledge that explained the importance of Giza, a structure built long before his time. Through a dream connection, Hermes shared this knowledge with Smoky Mirror, the dreamer of Teotihuacán, so there is a fundamental relationship between the size and form of the Great Pyramid of Giza and the Pyramid of the Sun at Teotihuacán.

Teotihuacán is a sacred site, one of the most powerful places on earth. Miguel says that the original spirit of Jesus resides in Teotihuacán, where he entered in his pure form as a beam of light. He and some of his followers sense that the spirit of the Christ resides in the Palace of the Jaguars behind the Palace of the Butterfly at the northern end of the Avenue of the Dead. Both Hermes and the Christ lent their power to Smoky Mirror. With their help, he recovered his own divinity and he designed a series of structures that would empower people to release the fears that keep them in the nightmare of hell.

Our long dream of hell has been filled with suffering, sadness, and anger. The quality of our emotions is controlled by our dream. If we change our dream from hell to heaven on earth, then the energy that the brain produces will be altered to vibrations of harmony and love. We might well ask, which comes first, the dream of love or the vibrations of love? The impulse which leads to a change of vibration in the human mind comes from the sun. The energy of the sun is pushing us to enhance love and reduce fear. We will find ourselves producing a different kind of dream, less of hell and more of heaven. The new dream began in the sun.

Miguel estimates that it will take two thousand years—the complete age of Aquarius—to totally change the dream of humanity, but the change has started and we are already being affected by it. Within his lifetime, Miguel anticipates he will see a crisis of transformation because the old dream will resist change. Regressive groups will want to cling to the power they gain by promoting the nightmare. Yet, fear has to be cleansed from our dream if we are to move away from the hellishness of the present state of humanity. A new dream cannot come in without the death of the old dream. This enormous, anticipated change will bring with it worldwide chaos which will follow the collapse of all systems based on fear. From chaos the new dream will grow and flourish. We have already begun this stage of evolution. All around us we can see the actions and reactions of change.

Trying to avoid change is a fruitless and unhelpful path. Change is inevitable. If humans do not make the decisions to change, natural disasters will make them for us. We have already had warnings of earth's impatience in recent floods, fires, and earthquakes, which can be interpreted as the earth healing herself of the wounds we have created. Troubled population centers attract natural disasters because the quality of the shared dream is more violent in densely populated areas. Miguel tells us that we can prevent disasters by being a little wise. A sign of changing consciousness can be seen in the exodus of people leaving huge cities to adopt a less destructive technology and a simpler lifestyle in smaller communities.

The wars that plagued the twentieth century were the result of our hellish dream, but humans are not necessarily warlike. As the dream changes, Miguel predicts that wars will eventually become only a distant memory in humans' minds.

Miguel's message is that we have nothing to fear. The way in which the world is evolving is just and right. Consciousness is changing and therefore evolution itself is changing. In the past, each major change in evolution was marked by a change in the energy sent from the sun.

The sun represents the active, masculine principle and the moon is linked to the feminine, intuitive principle. When we return to our pure state of energy at death, our destination is the sun. Going home means going back to the sun. The moon is an analogy for this return process. Just as the moon reflects sunlight back to its source in the sun, so individuals are able to metaphorically return to their source in the sun by means of the "smoky mirror" of the moon.

At Teotihuacán Smoky Mirror is a presence in the Pyramid of the Moon, with its great front plaza. The feminine aspect of this area is affirmed by a sixteen-foot high stone carving of a goddess weighing twenty-two tons that was removed from the plaza at the Pyramid of the Moon during major restoration work begun in Teotihuacán in 1962. It is now on display at the Museo Nacional de Antropologia in Mexico City. Although a similar, unfinished stone carving has been found near Texcoco, no other massive freestanding stone figure was discovered at Teotihuacán.

Archeologists have given the goddess personified in this work the Aztec name Chalchiuhtlicue, Goddess of Water and spouse of the God of Rain, Tlaloc. She once wore turquoise earrings and a jade skirt. Before it was stolen, she had a golden pendant in the center of her chest. Sitchin links the pendant to the search for gold that brought the gods to earth, but he agrees with other scholars that the Pyramid of the Moon symbolizes a reverence for the divine feminine. An equal reverence for water, symbolized by the Feathered Serpent and the head of Tlaloc, the Rain God, on the Pyramid of Quetzalcoatl, unites the major structures at Teotihuacán to symbolize the oneness of divinity. At Teotihuacán, these are the only deities who are portrayed, a male and a female.

The statue of Chalchiuhtlicue was discovered a century ago, lying face down among ruined temples on the west side of the plaza of the Moon. It was known as the "Fainting Stone" because people who lay on it were overcome with a feeling of lassitude. (See *Treasures of Ancient America* by S. K. Lothrop, page 41.) Now, separated from the vibrations of the other rocks and the pyramid, the statue seems alien and hard to read, but it was placed at Teotihuacán for a purpose. Even today, the work has meaning as a sign of our need to restore the feminine principal to our collective dream of God, and of the urgency that we protect water, which is like the blood of the earth.

At Teotihuacán, the dream and the gods were totally harmonious. This was truly the place where men could become God. During this time when the knowledge that is retained in sacred sites is coming into the minds of specially trained people, we again have access to the harmonious dream that once prevailed at Teotihuacán. Miguel's practice of returning to the trance state at this site, on monthly trips for five years, has inspired his interpretation of Teotihuacán.

Part of his work as a nagual, as Miguel Angel Ruiz sees it, is to penetrate the sacred purpose built into the pyramids and temples at Teotihuacán. Architecture and archeology alone cannot explain that purpose. Miguel's intention is to reclaim and to reenact the mysteries that were practiced at Teotihuacán centuries ago. The process of transformation was then and is now associated with the dream of entering a huge two-headed snake, manifested in the Avenue of the Dead.

The Avenue of the Dead ends at the Pyramid of the Moon where the pilgrim is symbolically disgorged from the snake. From there, the transformed seeker moves on to the adjacent Palace of the Butterfly, which symbolizes heaven, to be born again in a pure state of detachment and bliss.

Each step of the journey through the snake is meaningful. Before undertaking the process of liberation on the walk along the Avenue of the Dead, a person must become familiar with certain esoteric concepts that Miguel teaches. The next chapter is a review of key Toltec ideas that Miguel has recovered through his visions at Teotihuacán.

CHAPTER FIVE

MIND, EVOLUTION,
AND THE DREAM

I n Miguel's teachings he reiterates that all of our ideas and dreams come from the sun. We can only perceive things through reflected light which originates as sunlight. Reality as we know it is the re-creation in our minds of reflected light.

When the Bible says, "In the beginning was the Word and the Word was with God," it is both shamanically and scientifically true. Sound is akin to light and it has the same generative power as light. Sound is energy vibrating at varying speeds. Pure energy has the qualities of sound, color, temperature, motion, memory, and awareness. Life also possesses these qualities. Einstein, in his theory of the universe, compared energy with mass and velocity of light. The Toltecs made a similar observation in different words: "Everything is light. Everything we know is light based."

From an etheric standpoint, human life on earth was created in order to dream. Humans create the reality they perceive in their dreams. Whatever we perceive is a manifestation of our dream.

The transformation of energy into the dream begins in matter. The light we perceive reflected from a material object we then re-create as an image inside our eye, always indirectly. This process of perception involves our emotions. The images we re-create in our mind from reflected light are processed through our emotions and this activity develops our mind. Our mind is made from emotions, just as our body is made from atoms.

Miguel Ruiz:

At birth, the baby has no mind. It has the equipment — the brain — but it is immature. The child has to learn everything. The brain is a complex of blank computers. It is not conscious.

Although the newborn child has the cellular memory of evolution and a few emotions, it does not have the mind to create the dream.

The child is born with all the knowledge of the universe, but it cannot think. It just knows. Its DNA carries the silent knowledge of life. As soon as the neural system is developed in utero, it functions, but before birth it is not directly in contact with the light outside, only indirectly through the mother; therefore the child receives little of the information carried by light until birth.

For several years after birth, the child is still free like a wild animal. It is not domesticated yet and therefore it has not accepted the dream that is passed to it by its family, religion, and culture. As the child is domesticated, the development of its mind comes through emotions caused by punishment and reward. Gradually, the child learns all the rules of the system it inherits. It learns to behave in a certain way. It absorbs the dream of its society, but it did not choose the dream.

Domesticated youths usually rebel against the dream imposed on them. They are no longer innocent. In the Westernized culture that dominates earth, young people see violence everywhere. Violence is fashionable in entertainment and in the gangs that youths identify with in all parts of the world. The system of violence swallows them. They look up to accepted idols, such as the macho male and the female as sexual object. The criminal becomes a hero. The models our young people follow are hellish. They contribute to the nightmare that encroaches upon the world.

The woundedness Smoky Mirror saw around him continues today, but now the crisis affects the whole of society. We are looking for a better way to relate to one another. Matrimony, which is the basis of society, is now mired in a need to control; it must change to a relationship of respect.

At the end of the Piscean Age, we find that our collective dream is hell. We can see that it has poisoned us and the earth, and we assume that it is poisoning the universe itself. For the sake of the earth and the universe, the human dream is due for a correction as we move into the Aquarian Age. Changing our dream is an evolutionary step forward. With each Zodiacal Age or each Sun in Aztec terms, evolution progresses.

Evolution was directed for millennia toward the development of the human capacity to think, to dream, and to create reality. The next step is to grow beyond fear and into the practice of love. Love generates benign creative energy. We are discovering the energy frequency of love and its benefits in healing, education, politics, and spirituality.

The Judge and the Victim

There are two main rulers in hell—the Judge and the Victim. In our mind, our Judge blames us. Our Victim receives the blame and feels guilty. These two aspects of ourselves hate each other. Communication between them in each of us was broken during the process of our domestication, no matter which beliefs were held by the elders who raised us.

Miguel Ruiz:

Humans are domesticated animals. Before we were born, the dream of the planet already existed, with all of its rules, beliefs, and hopes. In the dream they are there waiting for the new humans to grow up and develop their minds in order to continue to control the dream. A pure, normal human being would be one who is still free, as he or she was in childhood before domestication, at the approximate age of one-and-a-half to three years of age. At that age, the child has developed enough mind to understand the abstract and to control language enough to communicate with other humans. However, the process of education has not yet taken place. This little human follows the normal tendency to play, to explore, to laugh, and to enjoy life. Almost all the child's emotions are coming from love unless he is angry or in pain. This little human is free to be and he lives in the present. He does not worry about the past. He is not worried about the future. The adults live constantly in the past and they are so worried in their effort to build their future that they avoid living in the present. For the adult, all the dramas of life are serious, but for the child nothing is really that important.

The dream waits to teach the small child how to join the old dream of the planet. Our parents, older brothers and sisters, our teachers, the school, religion, society, and the media all contribute to keeping the dream of the planet alive through domestication. Domestication comes through reward and punishment. Mom and Dad domesticated us just the way they were domesticated. They introduced us to the concepts of good and bad, by rewarding the good and punishing the bad.

Usually, when we feel the punishment we have the sense of injustice and we rebel. That opens a wound in our mind and the result of that wound is to create emotional poison. We feel that pain in our heart as an emotional, not a physical, pain. From this wound, the emotional poison gets into our mind. Fear begins and starts controlling our behavior and our mind. We become afraid of receiving punishment and we also fear not receiving a reward. The reward comes to be a sign of acceptance. We struggle to be worthy of it in the eyes of our parents, our teachers and friends, and society itself. Many times during the day as we grow up, we are subject to the judgment of others and to the polarities that our society supports, such as right and wrong, beautiful and ugly. Soon, we begin making our own judgments.

Domestication becomes so strong that we no longer need anyone to domesticate us because we take over the task of our domestication by punishing ourselves and occasionally by rewarding ourselves. Three components in our mind are actively engaged in our self-domestication. The Judge is that part of our mind that judges what we do, and what we do not do, what we feel and do not feel, what we think and what we do not think, and it also judges everything and everyone. The Victim receives the judgment and usually the Judge finds the Victim guilty. The Victim has a need to be punished. The Victim part of our mind feels unworthy and repeats over and over again, "I am not good enough, nor intelligent, nor strong, nor beautiful enough. I am a loser. Why should I try?" The third part of the mind involved in the judgment process is the belief system we have been taught which includes all the rules on how to dream our life. The belief system is a kind of constitution or holy book where everything that we believe without discussion is our truth. I call this belief system the Book of Hell.

The inner Judge bases all judgments in the belief system. Once we recognize this, we see that there is no justice in our own mind. If there were justice, we would pay for each of our mistakes once, but our Judge makes us pay a thousand times. We pay when we make a mistake and when we remember the mistake, or when anyone reminds us of the mistake. Each time, there is the Judge finding our Victim guilty and punishing us again.

Our belief system comes to us from society during the period of domestication. We absorb it from our family, the school, and religion. At no time does the small child have a choice of what to believe. Throughout the domestication process, the small child rebels, but he lacks the power to change anything. We rebel also as teenagers when we are searching for our identity. At this crucial time in our lives, we see how the belief system represses our normal human instincts and how adults manipulate young people. Depending upon how much resistance we meet during our teenage rebellion will be our future self-esteem. We might find some support and become a success in life, or we might succumb to fear.

The Judge, the Victim, and the belief system or Book of Hell are together a Parasite in our mind. The Parasite is a living being made from ethereal energy. To survive, the Parasite feeds on emotions that are created by the human brain. These are emotions that come from fear, anger, sadness, depression, jealousy, and victimhood. The Parasite controls the dream. It creates a dream of fear, a nightmare, in order to control the brain which is the factory of emotions. The Parasite controls the production of those human emotions which are necessary for its survival. At the same time, the brain stops producing the emotions it needs for the growth of the soul, which are the emotions that come from love.

The Parasite functions in a similar way to a virus which attacks a cell. The virus controls the reproduction of the cell so that it cannot produce the properties it needs for the cell's own growth. Instead, it produces what the virus needs for its own growth. The virus lives at the expense of the cell, and it damages the cell little by little until it is destroyed. We see all around us that human beings are engaged in self-destructive behavior. This is the outward sign of the self-destructive mind controlled by the Parasite.

The Toltecs were aware of the Parasite's existence and they knew that humans have only two choices in regard to this invasive force. One choice is to surrender to the Parasite, but the other choice is similar to that made by the little child and the teenager—rebel, declare war against the Parasite, and declare the freedom to be oneself, to have one's own dream, to use one's own mind, to create the emotions that feed the real person we are. The Toltecs, of course, chose to rebel. That is why they are called warriors. This is the real meaning of a warrior.

A warrior is that human who has the awareness of the Parasite in his or her own mind and declares a war on the Parasite for the purpose of self-healing. The importance of the war is not to win or to lose, but to try.

Every value system has its own Book of Hell. One book or the other is passed on in any family. The Judge and Victim are present in us regardless of the rightness or wrongness of the belief system we have absorbed. The warrior's task is to rebel against our inner Judge and Victim. By following the Avenue of the Dead at Teotihuacán in the Toltec way, the warrior can get beyond the Judge and Victim.

In every contemporary culture, there is an emphasis on suffering. A belief in suffering begets suffering. The Christian heritage teaches that it is necessary to suffer in order to copy Jesus. Miguel says this is a false dream or an illusion. Jesus himself preached that love was the answer to life. Placing a high value on suffering is just one example of beliefs that permeate our minds and our collective dream. In such phrases as "no pain, no gain," we reveal how deeply we have accepted the idea that we have no right to the joys of painlessness.

Even before we begin following the Avenue of the Dead in the Toltec way, we can do a mental exercise that is like an active prayer. The intention of the ritual is to become happy as we were meant to be.

Ask to die to the dream of the planet.

Prepare to leave hell.

Imagine yourself in heaven on earth.

CHAPTER SIX

TOOLS FOR TRANSFORMATION

PART ONE:
THE MITOTE AND THE INVENTORY

The Mitote

T here is an ancient practice among several Mexican ways of knowledge called the mitote. *Mitote* is an Indian word that has been adopted by the Spanish. The word means chaos, but it is used to signify a cacophony of voices without agreement, such as the gossip of a marketplace or the Tower of Babel. The Toltecs used to say that an ordinary human mind is a mitote.

Men of power and knowledge can be sorcerers. In the past, sorcerers took their apprentices to certain places where they partook of plants like peyote to stop their minds so they could understand that this reality is actually a dream. Today some sorcerers are still following this practice and it is called the mitote. Both the condition of being out of harmony and the practice used to clarify the confusion are called by the same name.

Miguel Ruiz:

The only way to harmony or heaven is to end the mitote. For the Toltecs, this refers to the chaos caused by the breakdown in communication within our own mind between the Judge and the Victim. The normal state of the mind is hell.

I conduct the practice of the mitote without drugs. I do not believe in drugs. I tell my students that we need to work together to end the mitote in order to change our way of life.

In the Toltec tradition, you face the mitote and do not deny it. The mitote is so powerful that we need help to disempower it.

We ask the Creator to help us and to give us clarity. We ask to receive courage to bring order to the mitote. In their practice of mitote, the Toltecs discovered that all knowledge comes to us. The mitote is an onion in our mind. We peel it back to find the lies and false images. When we have enough clarity and courage to go deeper, we find out who we really are.

We learn about all the agreements we have made and we see the possibility of shifting them. We learn to explore and control the dream. Mitote is not only a nighttime practice, but a day one, also. To do the mitote, we make it our intent to put order where there was chaos. Once you start the mitote, it becomes the purpose of life to replace chaos with order. This is the Way of the Warrior.

Today, in some places, the mitote is corrupted in its usage. For Toltecs, the first mitote is an initiation into the silent knowledge, but the mitote does not end at the close of the first ritual. I was initiated into the mitote in the desert with the teacher who was introduced to me by my grandfather.

The mitote goes through the night and ends at dawn, or else it lasts for two nights in a row. Doing the mitote means going into the space between sleeping and awaking. It energizes people so that they do not end the long mitote ceremony in a tired state.

During our mitotes with apprentices, in the center of the group, we have a fire, and the students take turns guarding it by staying awake. They are the Guardians of the Fire.

The other students begin chanting love and expressing love. It seems like a commotion at first, but then they take the dreamer position, sitting on the floor, wrapping their knees in their arms, and hanging their heads. They are wakened every fifteen minutes and change positions so a different person becomes the Guardian of the Fire. There are many chances to observe the exact moment when sleep begins. We guide the students to explore their dream by becoming aware of the exact moment when their brain goes to sleep. They must use their imagination.

The mitote is the Dreamer's Way. To do a mitote at home, I recommend you not try to do it alone. Your reason will try to sabotage you and it might bring on nightmares. Form a group and do it together. Ideally, you need a guide.

The Inventory

The inventory is that part of the Mastery of Transformation which challenges our belief system. The inventory is a review of one's belief system (which we have already described as the Book of Hell) where we have stored everything that we know. In making this review, the warrior recapitulates everything he believes. Miguel's students are instructed to make frequent personal inventories.

The purpose of the exercise is to recover one's free will. The inventory is your armament when you challenge your Parasite. The Parasite is a composite made of the Book of Hell, the Judge, and the Victim within your mind.

Look at your personal dream of life. Be honest with yourself. Are you happy or not? Your inventory will be based on the concept of happiness. The closer you are to happiness, the closer you are to the dream of heaven on earth.

Remember that your beliefs were given to you; you did not choose them. The beliefs that make you happy are worthy of being retained. The beliefs that cause you unhappiness can be reviewed and altered. Your goal is to reprogram your beliefs to achieve freedom from fear.

Free will is our right to make our own decisions. When we behave as a warrior, by using our free will, we have a second chance to choose what to believe. The problem we face is that our old belief system penetrates our entire mind. When we make our first review of our belief system, we do not see any space for new beliefs, but we make space for new beliefs each time we transform an existent belief.

The inventory is a very old practice from the Toltecs. It is a recapitulation of your whole life, of whatever has happened to you. It allows you to let go of all those beliefs that create the dream of hell.

The Breathing Technique
for Cleansing Emotions

Cleansing our emotional poison is a simple process. All it takes is the thought of love and our breath. We hold the wound in our mind briefly. Then we breathe deliberately while thinking of the word "love." We can apply this cleansing routine to old wounds and new ones. When we clean a wound, it heals itself. We cannot clean a wound by sharing the poison with someone else. Such an action increases the poison.

We are in a jungle full of poison that affects everyone. If you are attacked, just remember your attacker needs your energy. When you become a Master of Transformation, nothing will harm you nor will you find that you have interiorized any poison from others.

As you cleanse the wounds from your past, you will become alert in your daily life and no longer add emotional "baggage" to your soul. It will become habitual to cleanse your emotions everyday, if not immediately at the time they are felt, then later before going to sleep. In your review there is no Judge or Victim.

This concept has far-reaching implications for the field of therapy. In the Toltec way, getting rid of poison is a self-realized activity. It does not require a therapist.

Making the inventory brings into our mind all those beliefs and events in our life that carry emotional poison. Miguel teaches this breathing technique:

Miguel Ruiz:

Focus on your breath. Breathe in the love that is constantly in the air. Breathe in pure love. Breathe out pure love. Breathing is a direct connection with love. With your breath of love, cleanse each emotional memory as it arises.

Clear your mind. Stop your mind. Make it blank. Judge nothing. Train your mind to bring back your memories without thinking. Whatever you remember is significant. Trust the memory that comes.

Put your awareness in your will. The will calls forth the memory of emotions.

Pray into your will to bring up memories.

Variation of the Breathing
Technique for Women

After putting your awareness in your will, become aware of your heart.

Transfer the heartbeat to your womb.

Then transfer your will to your womb.

Now transfer your breath into your womb.

Start the inventory.

Let memories come spontaneously.

This process becomes even more powerful if you connect your womb with the full moon.

Recapitulating Your Dream

Now that you know the technique for cleansing your emotions, you can ask yourself, "What do I believe that makes me suffer?" You will start from that point. As each painful memory or guilt-causing belief arises, apply the cleansing breath to it.

Ask yourself, "How open is my belief system?" If your beliefs are held rigidly, you may feel afraid when you question or interpret your Book of Hell privately. It is for this reason that apprentices develop their awareness before they undertake the inventory.

Toltecs discovered the Mastery of Awareness when they became aware that this plane of life is a dream. They learned to observe the dream of the planet without any emotion and they recovered clarity of mind. Awareness and clarity lead to change. Change is possible if you make use of the Toltec masteries. See everything the way it is, then you have a chance. Awareness gives you an opening. By following this simple plan, you will begin your exit from hell.

We don't need to wait to go to heaven until we die. But we have to get there before we die. It is far easier to leave the dream of hell while we are living than it is after we are dead. Between us and freedom from hell, one of our traps is our own self-importance, with its pride and its fear of shame and punishment.

In recent years, many gurus are teaching others to blame their suffering on their parents, spouses, or other people. They are teaching their clients to be victims. The Toltec system teaches that we are no longer little babies, or helpless. We are strong enough to change everything. No matter what conditions you find yourself in, you have the power to change them. Even those who have been raped can change their reality. The effects of your wounds are lessened if you realize you are dreaming. You can change your inner movie because you are the director, writer, and actor, and you have all the power to change the story you are living.

Our sleeping dream usually continues our daydream from the same viewpoint as when we are awake. Our brain interprets what we perceive. The only part of the dream humans agree on is the frame. The frame is the same for all of us. The frame is the agreement we have made about our surroundings, our home on Planet Earth. It is the support that makes us feel safe and grounded. It gives us a sense of time and space. There are cycles of life all around us which create a sense of stability in us. We notice the changes in cycles of the moon, year, and seasons. Although the frame is not real, we just accept it, so we all see the same world. However, as soon as we interpret our experience, our dream becomes separate and private.

Miguel Ruiz:

We don't understand why we suffer. We don't realize we have a choice, but we DO have a choice. We are not totally responsible for the dream because it was here when we were born. In spite of the nightmarish dream, we are trying to make this a better place for our children. The dream of the planet has evolved through the millennia, so the dream is changing and the tendency is toward something better, but it is still a nightmare and it is still hell.

Our task is to use this lifetime to extricate ourselves from the dream. We cannot afford to wait for the dream to evolve into fearlessness. We must act for ourselves.

At first, it does not look as though we can leave the nightmare. The structure of the dream humans have created appears perfect.

Nonetheless, we don't have to suffer any longer. Once we are aware of the dream, we can attempt to get outside of it. Awareness makes it possible for a person to leave hell permanently.

We begin by noticing that we suffer for the little things we feel belong to us, that we need to control and defend. We can watch ourselves as we overreact to injustice. We can see ourselves in our need to have revenge and we realize there is no end to getting even.

Every human becomes a demon for the rest of humans and keeps the rest in hell. Each time we remember our partner's mistake, we make him or her pay again. Either the wife or the husband can become the demon through the act of revenge. We use a lot of emotional blackmail. We use guilt and blame to control the people that we love. We make promises. We fill our life with expectations and obligations. We have no eyes for real justice. Each person feels he or she is always right and everybody else is wrong. We believe our opinion is the most important.

We have to lie to ourselves and to everybody else. Everybody lies in this world. To say you are lying is not to make a judgment. It is just the way it is. Lying is a defense based on fear. We don't want to see our personal wounds, our anger and jealousy, or to see that we are afraid. We are playing with false images of ourselves in our lies. There is no communication between humans because of our lies.

As warriors we have come to the point of changing our life. We are going to transform it. We will stop the lies. We will give up our self-importance and exchange it for the freedom that comes when we make an inventory and use our cleansing breath to get out of hell. We will progress to making a new set of beliefs that do not cause suffering. This is a creative process like any other form of art. It takes an act of courage to start deliberately carving away any belief that causes you to suffer.

Perhaps you do not believe you have the power to make your own reality, but if you did accept this premise, you could then create a different reality from the one that causes you to suffer.

You will add those concepts that reduce your suffering to the new system that you are creating. As your personally created belief system grows, you will recover your birthright and regain the free will to make a choice whether to suffer or to be happy.

Until an inventory is made, you will lack the power to make the choice.

This inventory is only the first of many. On the Avenue of Death, you make a provisional inventory. On your personal path, you begin with a provisional inventory as well. It gives you enough power to continue on your way to freedom.

Remember that before you were domesticated, you were happy. You will try to recapture that happiness, not with the innocence of childhood but with the awareness of maturity. To search for God within is the purpose of Teotihuacán. It is like a map that will guide you to recognize yourself as God.

The Toltec system of the inventory is meant to bring about the recovery of your totality. You are incomplete as you are now. Continuous reviews of emotions and thoughts known only to you ferret out your fears and substitute love.

As you distinguish emotion-ladened memories in your mind, you will discover how many of your beliefs are reflections of other peoples' emotions.

▲ ▲ ▲

Become aware. Be honest with yourself. Know that you are in hell. Look at it. Don't deny that it is hell. Express what you are. Love others just as they are, whether or not they love you back. It is the love that comes from you rather than the love that comes to you that makes you happy.

Once you have awareness, you will find you have strong resistance to change because you have made an agreement with the dream of the planet and with yourself all your life.

When you were younger, you might have made an agreement to smoke. If you try to stop smoking, you might say, "I know all the reasons I should not smoke but I can't stop." It is the same with overeating. It is not easy to break an agreement that has been in effect for a long time.

The answer to discontinuing a habit lies in your personal will. To give up something, you need to put the same amount of power behind giving it up as you did to form the agreement to do it. To quit smoking, you have to make that your intention. You may have started smoking to be cool, to look older, to be one of the group. When you began the habit you now want to break, you invested your power in making the decision to take and continue to take this action.

Think of the effort required for a spaceship to break free of the earth. There must be a force exerted of sufficient strength to at least match the gravitational force that keeps the ship on the planet. It is the same in your personal efforts. You put a certain personal power in every agreement you have made and you need to put the same amount behind giving up the agreement.

Impeccability is the correct use of any kind of energy. By practicing impeccability, you can store up enough power to break your agreements. Use expands your power. After you expend your power to break an agreement, it will return and grow bigger. The inventory, or the Recollection, is a way for you to achieve power.

Miguel asks a person to make four agreements to study with him. He says that these four agreements will break eighty-five percent of your agreements that keep you in hell, but they do not work unless you practice. You accomplish miracles by practicing a little at a time until your power is strong enough to control all your agreements.

▲ ▲ ▲

Miguel Ruiz:

1. Be impeccable with your word. This agreement has deep meaning and it can take you out of hell almost by itself. The word is the strongest expression of the spirit. The word is the most powerful tool we have as a human. The word is divine. It is pure magic. It is pure power. Say only what you mean.

Real magicians manipulate the word in the best way and have the highest respect for the word. However, it is important to remember that each of us is a magician. We use the word to hurt each other, to blame, to blackmail, to gossip, gossip, and more gossip. Pure blackmail is destructive. With the word we keep each other in hell. Just by giving our opinion, we can build a person up or down. For instance, we say, "You're a coward." It affects the person for ages.

A little girl of six was singing as she played. Her mother had a headache and she had been having a hard day. The singing annoyed her. She went to her daughter and said, "Shut up. Your voice is like a crow. Shut up." The little girl won't ever sing again. She thinks her voice is ugly. Her mother has put a curse on her. We do this to many people. We give our opinion without thinking of the damage we cause.

The little girl made an agreement with herself, "My voice is awful." For her to break that spell, she must use the same amount of power to break the agreement. First she has to know how it happened.

Everything we do is based on agreements. An agreement is a binding force and it magnetizes energy to itself which adds to its strength and apparent correctness. The dream is based on agreements and so is suffering. Most agreements are limitations on ourselves. The inventory brings up our awareness of how we react in certain ways. We can then work out a way to break old, limiting agreements.

2. Don't take anything personally. We take everything personally when our personal importance leads us to make the assumption that whatever happens is because of us, which is why we continue to hurt each other and brood about what we call injustice.

3. Don't make assumptions. We make an assumption if we think that others know what we mean, or that we know what others mean. We have to have the courage to ask the other what he means, or what he wants, and the courage to say what we really want. Without assumptions, there is nothing to make you frustrated and there is no one to blame. You owe nothing to life and it owes you nothing.

4. Always do your best. When we always do our best, we avoid self-condemnation and we rarely become frustrated. When we are sick or tired, our best will be different from when we are well. Our best is always changing, but we continue to do our best. When we are fresh and healthy, our best is always changing. If we do our best under any circumstances, we will feel good about ourselves. In the inventory, you go into your mind and explore your belief system and find the agreements you have made and break them one by one.

Another way to become aware is to find the real dream and real dreamer. It takes courage to go into the dream. There is no safe place for the dreamer until you let go of reality and discover that you are the dream and the dreamer.

Clarity tells us this is nothing but the dream. If you can shift your point of view and control the dream you can create another reality. At first, it is difficult, but soon you find this reality less real. Afterwards, you will find it harder to adapt to what you formerly considered reality.

Toltecs combined both ways of becoming aware. They did the inventory and they also went into their dream. They knew that everything is a dream, so their goal was to become a dreammaster. They worked at gaining complete control of their personal dream until it obeyed them. Their goal was to be happy. They were no longer afraid to die. I teach the Toltec way of using both the inventory and the journey into your personal dream.

Toltecs are not ascetics. They have high respect for the material world. There is no need to be poor, or greedy either, in this system. You use the material world, but you know it isn't yours. Most agreements represent attachments. We say this is my body, my house, my family, my life . . . but it is not true. If you are afraid to lose your material or emotional acquisitions, that is hell.

As Toltec naguals, we give our body total control of the body. We let the body claim its personal power. We honor and love our body and allow our body to be just what it is without shame or revulsion.

We also honor our mind. We allow our mind to control the mind. The mind loves the body. We allow our body, our love, our mind, and our soul to be just what they are.

Chaos comes when the body feels "I am what I feel" and the mind feels "I am the body and I am what I think." To solve the chaos, let the body do the best it can, but not less than it can or more than it can.

Over time, inventorying becomes so automatic that the process can be carried on in dreams. Miguel has had the experience of an inventory of dreams in which all his old dreams returned. He felt it changed him as a person.

Miguel Ruiz:

All that earlier information was taken from my brain. I do not remember those dreams that came one by one, but I am a new man created from that inventory of dreams.

When we review the past, it is important to remember that the Judge and the Victim are unwelcome at the inventory. We must see the inventory with the eyes of love. If we review our life without love, we will reopen old wounds and create more emotional poison, and we will justify the pain we carry in our whole life.

Usually we store the events of our past in accordance with the interpretation we made of whatever happened. That interpretation will be keyed to our emotional state at that moment. Let's imagine that a couple has had a fight. The fight is witnessed by the mothers of the wife and the husband. It is also witnessed by a person who has no emotional attachment to either of the couple. The interpretation of the fight will vary in each of these five persons. The four who are related might write four different stories of the fight. The story closest to the truth will be that of the impersonal witness who lacks emotional connection to the participants.

It is likely that in making our own inventory with the eyes of the Judge and the Victim we will bring into our mind the original interpretation of the remembered event with all its blame and self-justification. This is why we try to assume the role of the impartial witness to our inventory.

We practice the special type of breathing when we do the inventory. We bring in love while doing the exercise. Whatever we recall, if we respond to it with love, we can transform even those memories we think of as injustices. With love we go into forgiveness. We forgive what happened and we forgive ourselves. The result is that our agreement changes and we recover a little more of the totality of ourselves.

Before beginning the inventory, a good technique is to write down a list of what it is you want to remember. Just writing things down as they come into your mind will initiate the process of remembering so you can recapitulate an event, an emotion, an interaction. You could speak your list aloud, but writing is more powerful.

You can make your list according to events, people, or dates. It is easiest to recall one person after another person as they came into your life, remembering as much about each one as you can. This is an effective way to review the interactions of your life. Eventually, you will do an inventory of your emotions. You can write lists many times. With every inventory you cut the hooks that keep you trapped in this reality. The fewer the hooks you have, the more power you accumulate for making your escape and developing your own mastery.

If you perform a recapitulation or an inventory each time you go to bed, you will add no more hooks. To do a daily inventory, just before sleep, pull your emotions back into your mind in a review of your day. When you waken at night, it is a good time to do an inventory. Force yourself to sit up and begin. Big inventories release your whole life of emotions, but everyday inventories of all your interactions and emotions are easier and faster than doing reviews of emotions long stored and unprocessed.

The inventory is a meditation exercise. An inventory is not an examination of conscience. There is no Judge nor Victim. It is a review of feelings. Ways to initiate this exercise might be: to put a candle in your room and look at it while focusing on your breath; to look deeply into a mirror; to sit in a darkened room with your feet on the floor and your hands in your lap; to lie down with a blanket over you with your hands crossed over your chest; or to sit on the floor with your arms wrapped around your bent knees while leaning back against a support. These are all techniques for going into a light trance state. They can enhance your power to make your inventory deeper.

Give yourself a command. "I am the Dreamer." Keep your eyes open. If you close your eyes, you will start dreaming, which is not the same thing as remembering. With your eyes open, your reason cannot deny what you are seeing. You need to convince yourself that you can see. You can go back to incidents of high emotion in your past as they come into your mind. After each inventory, you return to your dream of life with different eyes.

CHAPTER SEVEN

TOOLS FOR TRANSFORMATION

PART TWO

On this planet, all humans are hunters. Everybody becomes prey. You have a certain amount of energy. To survive and to grow, you have to acquire more energy. Wherever there is energy, whoever has it, you require it and by instinct you will try to take it.

The hunter is a stalker. The word as it is used in the Toltec tradition comes from the vision of the jaguar. The jaguar is a land animal who is always alert, always awake. It moves slowly to seize its prey. The jaguar sees accurately from close at hand. He lives in the present.

The stalker also includes the vision of the eagle. The eagle flies in the air with an overview of the scene. It does not see in great detail, but it can move directly to its prey. The eagle is the dreamer. By being the eagle with a panoramic viewpoint, it is easier to become a Master of Awareness, a hunter whose prey is the emotions. The eagle's viewpoint makes us quickly aware of our emotions, but they are harder to reach from such a distance.

The stalker can be like the spider who spins a beautiful web and waits for its prey. Humans hunt like a spider when they create situations that pull people into their web with charisma or with cunning. Human prey is always attracted by something it wants, such as power, position, and money.

The warrior is a stalker. When you become the stalker, you become the hunter, which means the warrior is the hunter who hunts power. You will stalk each of your emotions and every word that comes from your mouth. Once you begin stalking, you will learn to live in absolute freedom.

Stalking is a quest for transformation. On this quest, every action, thought, and spoken word takes on significance. For example, we might be in a conversation that becomes filled with gossip. To protect ourselves from this poison, we will have to cleanse the wound the gossip makes in us by using the breathing technique.

The warrior is the hunter who hunts for the power required to attain a level of mind that transcends the material plane. Power is a living being. This living being is the dream of the planet. Most human beings are working for this living dream, using all available power so the dream continues to grow. We trap our fellow human beings in the dream and we trap the new humans we bring into the world by teaching them to judge, to feel victimized, and to create poisonous emotions.

In the dream of the planet, the word is our most powerful way to spread poison. The word can destroy or save. Its effects ripple outward to an enormous extent. Through the word others force their poison on us. When we feel hurt or angry, we might say a word that has special potency. This is black magic. All of us are magicians trapped by the power of the word until we learn to stalk ourselves.

The highest achievement of the stalker is to become impeccable. You become impeccable when you realize that all you do is an act of power for which you are responsible. You almost escape the dream by developing impeccability, but it is still necessary to discipline your emotions. In order to be impeccable, you must stop spreading poisonous emotions or accepting them from outside yourself.

From Awareness to Stalking

The Master of Transformation must already have the awareness that we are multidimensional beings. This awareness is the prime requirement for becoming a Toltec Warrior. The Mastery of Awareness could also be called the Mastery of the Mind. However, it includes two points of view — not only the viewpoint of the mind, but also the viewpoint held by the physical body.

Miguel Ruiz:

Everything is a dream and only the dream exists. To explain ourselves and the world, we like to make divisions. The two main divisions are the dream and the dreamer. The dreamer dreams, yet the dream is there even without the dreamer because many other dreamers are maintaining it.

We adapt to the same frequency as the dream of the planet. The dream guides the dreamer, not the other way around. We are what we believe we are, but our position in the dream changes as our awareness changes. We become aware of how we dream and of our position in it. Once we are aware that everything is a dream, we discover the dream is a nightmare.

With Mastery of Transformation we can change the whole dream. It must happen at the personal level. Only by transforming ourselves, one person at a time, will the whole dream eventually be changed.

In history, we see that human beings have always searched for eternal happiness. We seek a state of grace or a state of bliss in heaven or Nirvana or Olympus. With the kind of dream that dominates this planet, it seems impossible to reach our goal of happiness. The Toltecs knew how difficult it is to be happy. They explored how to change the dream and they discovered the first two masteries: The first is awareness and the second is personal transformation.

The major tools we use to develop Mastery of Transformation are stalking and the inventory (which is also called the recapitulation). I think of the inventory as an art of dreaming, and the art of the eagle. We use our memory to go into our past and recover it. Therefore, we would say that the inventory is about the past, whereas stalking is about the present. The art of stalking is the art of free will, choices, and taking risks. It is the art of being alive, always in the present like the jaguar.

The way to control the dream when we are awake is by making choices. Throughout the universe, there is a process of action and reaction. The dream reacts to our choices. The art of stalking has to do with our control over our reactions. We begin by stalking our actions.

Here, we must return to the theme of domestication. Domestication taught us how to dream and to adapt to the dream of the planet. It programmed our mind with a whole belief system. It provided us with our position in the dream, in our family, in the community, and in ourselves. Our position is the image we hold of ourselves at any moment. Our position is what we believe we represent in any situation. In every position we take we attempt to prevail, and everyone else is also trying to prevail. This leads to chaos and confusion.

Our dream and our position in that dream are the results of what we believe we are. This belief is controlled by emotions, not by reason. Reason feels victimized because our experiences are not logical.

Everything we experience has an emotional component. We react emotionally, for example, to beauty. The emotional body has only one purpose and that is to feel. The intellect makes an interpretation of what we feel and attempts to justify our emotional reactions. The intellect tries to repress the emotional body and to cover our wounds with lies to avoid pain. In this way, we develop our denial system.

We begin denying our experiences as a little child when we react to what we consider to be injustices. The interaction between the emotional body and the intellect creates a growing conflict and a lack of self-acceptance. Mainly, we don't accept our emotions. Particularly in Western society, we are embarrassed by our emotions and we often deny them.

When we are alone, we really believe in the image of what we think we are. This image is not real. It is a part of our dream. It carries the guilt and blame that are remnants of our domestication process. Many of us hate ourselves so much we cannot enjoy life. To be honest with ourselves and to uncover the lies we have been taught to believe takes courage. The process of opening our wounds is painful, but this is what the Master of Transformation does when he or she stalks.

When we are awake, the art of stalking consists in always being alert to our thoughts, actions, and reactions. The novice begins by focusing inward. We always begin with ourselves. From this self-study, we can understand others who are doing the same thing we are doing based on their own belief system. When we are asleep, the art of stalking gives us control over the dream of life. We can become dream masters.

The stalker uses free will to make choices and does not rely upon emotions. By letting the Judge and the Victim decide things for us, we give up responsibility and we lose our free will. The stalker deliberately takes his or her choices back from the Judge and Victim.

Life is always action. Action makes the difference in the world. The stalker can make a dream come true in material reality. The dreamer cannot do that. The stalker has the power to change the outside dream within the limits of his position in that dream. The dreamer is unable to do this.

After stalking within and gaining mastery, the new master nagual starts stalking the outside dream of the planet, which is that dream shared by all humans.

Once the stalker has a cleansed mind, he or she can begin expressing to the outside dream. As the dream changes for one stalker after another, we will see that there is no place for poverty or for the passive acceptance of degradation. Action creates abundance.

A master is almost finished with the inner work of transformation when he or she starts to create in the outside world. Like a doctor or an engineer, we become experienced before we can practice what we have learned. In terms of the study of Toltec mastery, one must transform all one's inner wounds to get rid of self-destruction. One must heal the dark side of one's nature. The emotional body is filled with wounds and is starving for love and justice. Once these wounds are healed, the transformed warrior expresses only love. The Master of Transformation is also a Master of Love, or we might say a Master of Intent. These are synonymous terms. The warrior learns that the truth is love.

To Learn the Art of Stalking

Miguel takes a sequential approach when he teaches the art of stalking. He continuously restates these core ideas:

Miguel Ruiz:

We must remember that we are humans who are in hell, trapped by the dream of the planet.

We use stalking as a tool to acquire awareness, change our dream, and escape from the dream. The stalker in ourselves helps us to stop the nightmare and to start getting into position for an escape from hell.

In our normal state, we have the idea that we are here to suffer for our whole existence. We dream the nightmare and we develop a faulty memory. We can barely remember yesterday. We think we know a lot about ourselves, but the truth is we know hardly anything about ourselves.

Last night I spent the whole night dreaming of power but I cannot remember the dream. I know only that it was about power.

I remember a few things about when I was eight years old in second grade, but I do not recall what I said and did then. Illusions blind us. We live in a false environment that causes amnesia. There are whole parts of myself I do not know. It is the same with each of you.

I present this sequence of concepts to my apprentices who are becoming Masters of Transformation:

1. We are born in this world with a certain amount of energy encased in an egg. The egg houses our body and all spiritual energies that surround the body.

2. We have a physical body at birth, but we develop a mental body after birth. Although the newborn baby has no mind, its soul can be strongly felt.

3. In order to grow, we take in energy from the outside world. We need to feed our various bodies with different kinds of energy. The physical body needs food, but that is not the only energy we require to grow. We are like a living being that needs to grow into a fruit.

Some other being will use the fruit for its own food. Our fruit is our awareness. Every kind of energy has awareness, but human awareness is separate and different from the awareness of other beings in this and other realities. Our human awareness is knowledge.

4. With our mind we create energy. The collective mind pressures our inner mind to create energy. Fear teaches our mind how to dream.

5. Reason connects our inner dream to the outer dream. Reason gives us its own special awareness. It is not the same as the body, mind, or soul awareness, nor is it like any other energetic system that is human.

6. Awareness grows through personal importance. Reason encourages our sense of personal importance which creates a false position or image of ourselves. From our false image, we create the fruit that is awareness. Then we discover the value of reason that produces its special awareness.

7. Reason stores a huge amount of energy. Many other organic and inorganic systems around the level of human awareness feed on our stored energy.

8. We derive energy for our awareness by absorbing it from other humans or from the dream of the planet itself. The dream of the planet loans us its energy. Later it will claim the final product—our awareness. The dream of the planet makes an investment in our growing awareness in order to take the fruit. This is like planting a seed and later eating the fruit.

9. For the dream of the planet and other energy systems around the planet, human awareness is very valuable. This explains why there are so many humans.

10. The dream of the planet pays for the fact that human awareness is destructive. At a certain point, human awareness goes out of control. Many other energy systems then try to control the production of humans. At this time we can see that human awareness is like a cancer out of control from points of view other than human. We are destroying the environment of our planet. Humans need to be stopped, but at the same time there is an abundance of the fruit of human awareness, which means there is an abundance of energy.

11. From the outside, we can see the huge living being that is the dream of the planet which enslaves humans to work for the dream. Humans are trapped in this reality and it is difficult to escape. The relationship of the human to the dream of the planet is a form of symbiosis.

The dream of the planet provides the energy for human growth, but the price is high. There is no freedom. Humans live in slavery on Planet Earth.

12. Dying is not the way to escape. The body dies but the soul continues and it can be trapped by the energetical system of the earth. When the body dies, the dream of the planet takes that part which belongs to it. Little by little, it absorbs all the emotions that belong to the dream. Other emotions remain with the soul and the reincarnation plan of the soul.

13. When a new cycle begins, the process is repeated: the loaning of energy, growth of awareness, and claiming of that awareness by the dream of the planet.

Souls remain trapped in earth's environment life after life until they learn the art of stalking.

Self-Love and Transformation

Miguel Ruiz:

Always look first for happiness. Happiness can come only from inside us. No one can make us happy. Happiness is an expression of our love coming out of us. We are not happy because others love us, but because we love them. The purpose of Toltec training is to convince a person to love herself or himself.

Everything is here so that we may love it, including ourselves. When our love for ourselves is conditional, our love for others is also conditional. Through our woundedness, we first deny ourselves love and then we deny it to others. Therefore, self-love has to be the first goal. If you have enough self-love, you do not need the love of another person. You can enter a relationship because you want to do it, not because you need it. If you are needy, you can be manipulated. If we are happy, we do not need another person to make us happy. We share our happiness, not our loneliness. Self-love makes us lovable. Others always move toward the person who is at peace with himself or herself.

Miguel tries to make people aware of the blocks in their lives that come from their belief systems. Naguals play tricks on their apprentices to help them loosen their blocks. Firewalking is a trick to bypass the belief system. It opens possibilities to the apprentice stalker. The goal is to stop being rigid.

The *position* we assume in any situation is our way of dealing with circumstances. Our position is always changing. When we think of ourselves with detachment, we are free to change our position from moment to moment in a graceful spontaneous response to circumstances, without self-judgment. We become aware that we are always acting. We are all wearing masks. We can shift in any way at all. Such awareness could lead to duplicity and chicanery, but when a person has cleansed all wounds first, then the self-awareness becomes a powerful tool for remaining free of the dream of the planet.

In the ancient days of the Toltec at Teotihuacán and Tula, and in the Mayan cities, many masks have been found. These masks were not only an art form of the Toltecs, they were a purposeful part of the teachings. The masks were hung on the wall and the apprentice would stand in front of one mask and practice making the same facial expression until he or she could feel the same emotion that the mask expressed. At first, the apprentice only aped masks without eyes. Then, with increasing proficiency, the apprentice moved on to imitate the expression of masks with eyes.

The practical use for this discipline was to send apprentices into town to study the facial expressions of ordinary people.

The face in repose is the real face of a person. With mastery, the Toltec could analyze the condition of the person in much the same way as another might study an aura. Great precision in understanding human beings was developed through this practice. A master needed only a glance to know the feelings behind the expression on a face. By copying the expression, the master could experience the emotions of another person. It was especially useful in determining if someone was lying.

Many people in the world instinctively wear an appropriate mask to achieve the result they seek. However, this is shamanic knowledge, part of the silent knowledge, and it is properly taught only to dedicated apprentices. It gives a person a power that could be misused.

In the stalking process, we come face to face with our positions in all the varied circumstances of our life. Some of these positions cannot be changed. One of the positions that cannot really change is that of one's gender. If you are a woman, no real change of that condition is possible. Sometimes in our inner dream, we do not accept these unchangeable things. This leads to an avoidable misery. Once you transform the inner dream, you can accept your unchangeable positions with greater equanimity.

Miguel Ruiz:

Other conditions may be difficult but you could change them. Perhaps you are a Persian woman living in Iran or Iraq. You could work on this condition. You would still be a woman but you could modify your position in relation to your location in that culture. If you should do so, others who notice your behavior might alter their situation also.

Not all modifications end happily. Hitler is one who tried to modify the outside dream by making it even more hellish. Mahatma Ghandi, on the other hand, first cleansed himself and then his actions in the world were effective and benign.

Toyland

Toyland is a metaphor Miguel uses to teach apprentices to appreciate themselves just as they are, with detachment.

Miguel Ruiz:

I sometimes speak of The Toy who lives in Toyland. If you think of the whole world as Toyland, your body becomes your favorite toy. You love your body. Without your body there is no action. Your body was made to have fun, not to suffer and not to win a contest. With your body, you can speak and share what you are dreaming. You can see the outside world. In Toyland you will have gratitude for your body and you will respect it. Anyone who wants to play with your toy has to regard it as highly as you do.

In Toyland everyone wants to be happy. All the toys who live in Toyland are playing a game either alone or with others. Anyone can change games at will. Every toy has its own ability, so the result of the game depends on how each of us plays. In Toyland, you can be a doctor, an engineer, whatever you want. You practice playing and rediscover the emotions you knew as a child when anything was possible. Your imagination helps you regain personal freedom. Morality is higher in Toyland than it is in the hell that is the outside world. In Toyland, you can change your position at any time, so there is less emphasis on defending a position. When two toys marry, they both can seek happiness without interfering with the freedom of the other. The idea of Toyland works well to allow for detachment from entrenched positions. It encourages the self-acceptance of knowing that what you are IS.

With stalking, you control your dream and you can make any dream you want. Because everything is an illusion, stalking can be a game, like in Toyland. We only suffer when we do not have the courage to change our game or our position, in order to release ourselves from the game that we do not want to play. In Toyland, we are encouraged to find out what we really want and then to create a game to make it possible.

A Toltec apprentice warrior must reach the mastery of being a toy. This discipline lowers one's self-importance and allows the apprentice to witness the comedy in life rather than the tragedy most others see. Apprentices learn to let go. A stalker has to take risks. Stalking is like a game in which you have nothing to lose.

Over the years that I have taken apprentices, I have seen the results of their mastery of stalking. One student of Toltec wisdom has become a writer about business. He gives seminars around the country. After a short period of chaos in their minds, the successful masters have gone on with their lives and their work. Toltec wisdom is a continuing process. There is no time in which one could say, "Now, I am finished with all this practice. I am a nagual." Becoming a master is a way of life and a lifelong pursuit.

Stalking the Body

Miguel Ruiz:

We have been speaking of the art of stalking from the point of view of the mind. The other point of view we want to address is that of the body. One of our most vulnerable wounds is our judgment of our own body. Our body is our most loyal, trusted friend. The Toltec way is to honor the human body, to keep it as clean as possible, and to think of it as perfect just as it is, but most of us find this attitude difficult to maintain. Most diseases of the body are derived from a mental state that is dependent upon our position in life. Disease often comes from avoiding responsibility for our own health and trying to justify ourselves as victims.

Negative opinions about the body affect the mind and then the mind represses the body. In this way, the body gives power to the mind. Some of the body's involuntary movements as well as voluntary movements are ruled by the mind. The mind thinks, "I am my body." The mind divides the body's needs into acceptable and unacceptable. The mind interprets the body's needs as the mind's needs. The mind always wants quality and quantity, so even if the body is already full, the mind might perceive that the body needs to be fed. The Judge in the mind compares the body to an ideal unfavorably and blames the body for "needing" food. The mind thinks of the body as guilty and yet it is the mind that causes the body to overeat.

We aspire to change our treatment of our body. The best we can do is to respect the limitations of our body, to see the beauty of the body—our own and other people's. At each age, at each stage, however it looks, we can find its beauty.

Our body belongs to the Angel of Death. It is only on loan to us. We can develop gratitude for all of its parts and all of their functions. In contrast to the more Puritanical beliefs in our culture, the Toltecs believe that our gratitude should extend to our reproductive organs and the power they give us to bring in new children.

If we become aware of gratitude and build our respect for our body, without possessiveness, this awareness will do eighty percent of the work to bring our body into a more ideal form. Perfection is already here. We don't need to work for perfection.

We can monitor our way of seeking the opinion of others. When we doubt our own opinion of our body, we ask others, "How do I look?" One negative opinion can destroy our inner view of ourselves. When we do this, we give away our power in our need for acceptance. We also stimulate our Judge and Victim.

The needs of the body and the needs of the mind are two different things. Physical exercise allows the body to recover its own power. In the Toltec training of the nagual, exercises begin with the technique of joyous breathing. At the beginning of this book there is a prayer to ask for a reconnection with the love that is in the air itself. Becoming conscious of the love that is available each time we breathe is a goal of the apprentice warrior.

The Physical Regime
of Transformation

Miguel Ruiz:

Although I will not go into them in this book, I do teach a series of physical exercises that are similar to the martial arts, yoga, and Tai Chi. The reader can practice any system of exercises because the purpose of exercising is to create a flow of energy through the body without blockages. Exercises bypass the many negative opinions most people have developed about their own bodies and they empower the body. When you do exercises, begin by contemplating the pleasure of being alive.

We are multidimensional beings and our bodies are composed of multidimensional organs. We need to honor our hearts, our lungs, our intestines . . . all parts of ourselves. Each part of our body has its own awareness. We begin our exercises with a prayer, which puts us in a state of gratitude for our body.

As we exercise, we hold postures and we breathe consciously. I always tell my students to find their own rhythm of breathing. I do not direct the rhythm, as is done in yoga. Each of us has a different rhythm that we are comfortable with. Your muscles and joints also have a rhythm. When you exercise, always listen to your body. Attempt to awaken each part of the body and to recover its well-being. Let go of the emotions stored in different parts of your body. The purpose of this kind of exercise is not to develop strength but to release emotions and to achieve inner harmony by ridding the body of toxins. As the emotional toxins are released, a harmony develops between the organs and a total energy flow among the chakras. Chakras usually refers to the seven energy centers found from the crown of the head to the base of the spine along the central axis of the body. The concept originates with the Hindu and the Buddhist systems.

While you exercise, hold the posture and explore the intent of the movement. The movements in all exercise systems express the beauty of the human body. In each position, the body is like a statue. Exercising with this in mind is an art. Begin a program that is very simple. I teach a sequence of exercises for revitalizing the whole body that takes an hour and a half. When done as a discipline, the exercises have a weight loss effect.

I stress the connection between our bodies and Mother Earth. The four elements of earth, air, fire, and water are represented in the exercise system I use. The human body is earth. The spine, the brain, and the nerve system are fire. The circulatory systems are water and the lungs are the air.

The regime I teach begins with fire breathing. Think of two main centers of the body, the bottom of the spine and the pineal gland, which connect with the element of fire.

The pineal gland in the center of the forehead area is light sensitive. It is the point of connection between our body and the sun.

To do fire breathing, suck in air with a gargling noise at the back of your throat. Blow out air between your teeth with a shushing noise.

Inhale a breath from the sun, through the pineal gland to the base of the spine. As you inhale, visualize going to the center of the earth and giving yourself as an offering or a communion.

Exhale while visualizing that you are bringing the answer from the earth and sending it to the sun.

Through our breathing, we make an invitation to the sun and to the earth to join in our body. We unite the two energies of the sun and the earth.

Our nerves have direct contact with every cell in our body. Our breathing energizes and revitalizes every cell of our body. It takes healing to each cell. As you breathe, you can feel the flow of energy moving throughout the body.

I learned this exercise system from the teacher I knew in the desert during my year of internship after medical school. You will see little statues in Mexico that demonstrate the poses he taught me. The same movements are found all over the world because all people have discovered the power of the movements.

During the meetings I hold with apprentices, we also exercise the voice with chanting.

Our purpose is to recapture the pure, elemental nature of sound. Silence gives form to sound. Humans are artists of sounds in language and in music.

We practice the impeccability of the word in which we use the word constructively. We stalk the word and we become conscious of the power in the words that we say. We notice the power behind opinions, the effect of judgment and blame. If we speak from a place of healing, our words will lose the power to wound others. When we react with pain to the words of others, we find our wounds. We search our memories to find the source of the pain the words recalled. Then we can heal the wound.

Once these devotional practices are learned, there is no need for anyone to attend a class to do them. They can be done at any time. While waiting at a stoplight, a person can practice fire breathing. In the midst of housework, one can hold a statuesque pose and breathe consciously. The purpose of all the training is to become conscious in the present moment.

Testimonials from Stalkers

Bernadette Vigil, an artist who has apprenticed with Miguel, is now a fully-trained nagual. Miguel has assured her it is time to take her own groups to Teotihuacán and to teach her own apprentices. When she explains what becoming a nagual means, Bernadette says, "I have forgiven myself. I have given up the role of victim. My emotional body has died. It died during the ceremony in Teotihuacán." She speaks of the assemblage point, which is that point in each of us where we can access our silent knowledge. As we gain in awareness, the assemblage point can shift and expand, which results in increased awareness.

Bernadette explains her feelings as a stalker: "In order to be impeccable, I'm very cautious about what I say and what I think. When I teach, I shift my center to bring in the total nagual, which is in other dimensions. The nagual is part of an individual's total being, but it extends further into other dimensions than merely the spiritual body. We begin our stalking class with a prayer circle. We place our intent aloud and listen to one another. Silent knowledge comes in, bringing a huge amount of energy into the circle.

"I sense the assemblage point of new apprentices to be at first slightly to the right on the back of their spiritual bodies. Acting as a nagual, I touch the new student while I am in a trancelike state. I channel energy from my will to their will. Each student begins to realize that he or she already has silent knowledge.

"The mind is made by billions of emotions. Every emotion is a living being, which all together create the mind. The mind is like a country where there are millions of humans. You must ask, where and who is the leader of this emotional country? Stop all judgment and refrain from talk of abuse. To think about being abused is to accept being a victim. In the Toltec tradition we disavow being a victim.

"At Teotihuacán, each step along the Avenue of the Dead is a preparation for dying by letting go of fear. At one point, you bury the self that you have been. Walking this route compares with climbing the chakra ladder in the Hindu system. Each step brings more awareness as you surrender your fears."

Bernadette speaks of the egg that houses the soul. Our body is not our border. Beyond the body is spirit, which is enclosed figuratively in an egg. Those with special gifts have a double egg surrounding the body. Miguel has found that most of his apprentices have the double egg and Bernadette has found this among her apprentices also. A student who lacks the double egg can break the single egg and create a double egg when nagual energy enters his or her field—an event that can be almost instantaneous for a fully committed student.

Miguel's wife, Gaya Jenkins Ruiz, who is also a nagual woman and a teacher, reminds us that the definition of relationship is "touching each others' wounds."

"If someone comes to you and says something that affronts you, and it stays in your mind, then there is something in you that needs to be cleansed.

"We vibrate at certain frequencies. If you are carrying a pocket of anger and you interact with Jane, you are sending your anger to Jane. The anger hits Jane's auric field. If she also feels anger, your anger will activate hers. However, if Jane is not feeling angry, she will not be vibrating at the same frequency and what you send out will just flow through her.

"We do not need to protect ourselves from anyone. We only need to protect ourselves from ourselves. If something affects us, it probably stirs our sense of personal importance. We become vulnerable when our ego is stirred. A feeling of insult or upset is a signal that our personal importance is still active and needs cleansing."

Gaya reminds students that if you watch your thoughts and your desires everyday, and then, when you go to bed, you say a prayer, it strengthens your control when you enter your dream state. One of Miguel's students speaks of the restraint the habitual inventory has on your inner nature. "You realize immediately, oh, now I'm going to have to recapitulate all this stuff. If I have a conversation with someone and I see there is no need to have the conversation except to express my self-importance, I start to become very economical with my energies."

That attitude, Miguel agrees, is impeccability.

Another of Miguel's apprentices presented his own view of stalking, which he compared to having the point of view of an artist. The stalker, he said, is a Master of Awareness. As he grew more adept at stalking, he started paying attention to color, to the way his room is arranged, the way his life is arranged, and how he interacts with his family. It was like seeing power in the form of beauty for the first time. "A huge doorway opened up for me. All of a sudden, it was as if life could be fun," he said.

He recommends that a student of this wisdom take whatever shred of awareness is available and modify it, make it grow, and concentrate upon the quality of beauty. There is power in beauty and joy in aesthetics in general. The hunter is looking for something personal to fill a need. For the stalker, the personal need falls away a little bit as something deeper begins to grow, which cannot be controlled with the intellect. You find yourself being pulled towards beauty, but it is different for every individual. By following your intuition, you gravitate toward that beingness, that silent knowledge you are seeking. This wisdom is larger by far than the sense of self, and it arises in a place of deepest desire that your soul has always yearned for. You knew the desire in child-hood because a child still has a vital connection with soul. The stalker finds that certainty again.

A woman who claims to be a dreamer finds that stalking makes her more aware of action. It also prevents her going into her own pain. It helps her to make decisions. By stalking she is becoming more self-aware and she enjoys doing it. She questions her emotions. "Why am I feeling uncomfortable? I try to find where the feeling is coming from. Is it my own fear for my security, or is it because I don't like the situation I am in with other people?"

When she is in a dream state, a female apprentice explains, she can be watching an action occur, be aware of it, and pull away from it, detach herself from it, and then create from that or make things happen from that crossover of two kinds of awareness at once.

A stalker is fearless. A stalker knows what it wants and goes for it. Before acting, in the middle of acting, or after acting, the stalker tunes into its intuition and listens. Then, the stalker will let nothing get in its way.

"For me," another woman says, "being a stalker is just being aware and observing my actions at every moment of my life. It is being conscious of what masks I wear and when and how I wear them. Again, it's really tuning in to my intuition and trusting the proper way to be when I am challenged. At times, I wish I were a dreamer because I am constantly confronting living as a stalker. Yet, I'm glad I am aware and really present to observe everyone and everything that happens."

A man adds the observation that the art of stalking is also referred to as the art of transformation. "I use stalking to pull myself out of hell. I use stalking to wage the battle between the Judge and the Victim. So, stalking allows me to be aware of the energies in my body that are not helping me to be what I really am. If I observe that I am feeling anxiety, I realize it is only because I am not in the moment. As soon as I bring my attention back to the moment, the anxiety is gone. Because I am able to observe what I'm feeling at any given time, I have the power to change it. If my power is great enough at that moment, I can pull myself out of hell.

"My assemblage point shifts to that anxiety, and I become aware of it and shift it back by will. Without stalking I am not aware that I have shifted to a place that is not where I want to be. Stalking is the tool that has allowed me to be a happy person. Without stalking I could never experience love or life. I would have stayed behind my veil of shyness. The stalker in me is very strong and it says, 'To hell with the fear. I'm going through it.' In order for the stalker to be effective, you have to be extremely relentless. Otherwise, there will always be an excuse to stay stuck."

"We usually talk about stalking versus dreaming, but that is only at one level of explanation," adds a woman. "When you go beyond that, stalking is dreaming. Once we are aware, we realize we are always dreaming. When someone says, 'I am a dreamer and I don't know what stalking is,' I think, 'Well, you have to stalk or else you would not be connected to this dream.' You have to choose whether you are stalking in awareness or not. If there were a pure dreamer who did not stalk at all, the person would be floating all the time. The person would not have a clue what is going on, what his or her name is, what day it is. All actions that we take or the direction we turn our attention to, that is stalking . . . stalking the dream. At any given moment, there are an infinite number of things we can give our attention to. What we choose to put our attention to tells us what kind of stalker we are. I wanted to point out that stalking and dreaming work hand in hand though they seem contradictory. The stalker is that part which observes with awareness and detachment from the dream you are in. You are caught up in the dream but you are detached from it. The stalker is able to unhook itself from an emotion or from the dream."

One male apprentice describes stalking as an evaluation of energy. If we are not to judge, we have to have some method for evaluating. Rather than judge, we can evaluate the energy in a person or a situation in terms of how appropriate it is to our actions, to ourselves. Some energy will not be important to you, but other energy will connect closely with what you are trying to accomplish. You have to make evaluations in order to be a stalker moving toward a goal. There is a difference between surrendering yourself to spirit and surrendering yourself to the domestication of old habits. It is sometimes difficult to delineate when you are involved in a project, whether you are doing what you want to do or whether you are doing what spirit has contoured for you. You cannot separate stalking in the outside world from stalking yourself. Every action you take on the outside path is mirrored on the inside path. Stalking is an evaluation of your energy and an alignment of your spirit energy.

Miguel Counsels His Apprentices

Miguel Ruiz:

When you come into the world, you become trapped here in a position of being emotionally dead. You are neither happy nor unhappy until you develop your personality for dealing with the world. Usually, you choose a mask with different variations. The mask makes a person feel safe. The mask is the modality that the stalker shows to the world. When you decide, as a child, how you are going to be in the world, this decision will affect your entire life. As a teacher, the nagual tries to discover which masks his or her apprentices are using in order to understand the mode or quality in which they try to deal with the world.

If you can see beyond the masks people wear, you can choose your actions when you interact with them. Your interactions will be more effective when you stalk. Just reacting to circumstances and people in the same old way is not effective. Stalking in the business world would be far more effective than being a pawn caught up in the system. Stalking and seeing clearly give you a tremendous advantage and they protect you from being pulled into the hell of the business world.

Stalking is a way to go into the higher realms and bring back help to lift human beings to a higher state of awareness.

Once you have cleansed your emotional poison, someone can come to you with rage and you will not receive it. This happens when you become masterful. You can say to yourself, "I'm going to stay in love," and it will affect the other person to notice that you are not changed by his rage. Mastery means not being affected by other people's poison.

There will be continuous temptations. Other living beings will tempt us back into the dream through their manipulation of our emotions. They are responding to the dark light of Lucifer as he is described in scripture. With mastery we can stay clear of the tempters. Jesus showed us how to resist temptation with love. You do not try to stop emotions of rage, you just let them flow through you.

In Teotihuacán there is an ancient residential compound one and a half kilometers from the Pyramid of the Sun, close to the River San Juan, called Tetitla. Tetitla means "Place of Stones." Many murals have been found there.

Tetitla is a place of pure black light. This is a healing energy which goes into the wounds we carry around with us and clears away the poison from them. The black light is pure love, or the love that purifies. Even the wounds that you do not know you have, based on childhood fears, will be released in this light. False images will break down. Anger may change to sadness, which is just a symptom of the cleansing you will experience as you allow yourself to express an emotion for the first time after many years of repressing it under a mental image.

The experience of going to Tetitla is archetypal, a prime example of the cleansing process. If one cannot go there, the experience of cleansing can be brought about by your internal inventory.

As a person of perception, you have different points of view that can perceive different rates of energy. The assemblage point makes fluctuations in the will, from deep in the will to the surface of the human "egg." The assemblage point is the place where you perceive this reality. Emotions of anger, jealousy, and fear occupy only a small range in this point of view. From other parts of your total point of view, you do not perceive them. It is possible to move out of the range at which they can be perceived until you have almost no connection with this reality at all. If you think of your chakras as your perceptual windows, you can imagine that from each level you will have a different viewpoint. Perhaps from the base chakra and the gonad chakra some of the same information is perceivable, but from the base chakra one could not perceive all that one could from the gonad chakra. You have a customary assemblage point, somewhere within the spectrum of total awareness. It is not wise to try to alter this assemblage point until you have rid yourself of fears.

All efforts in the Toltec tradition are directed to raising your personal awareness away from the fear-driven old dream of the planet to the new dream of heaven on earth. However, the old dream is now thousands of years old. It is deeply entrenched in the minds of all humans. The dream itself is a living being. It is an archangel that came from the sun.

Spirit is pushing us to change the dream. Spirit is reclaiming his kingdom. When we entered the Sixth Sun, it gave us an opportunity to make this change in the dream. More than an opportunity, it was a command from the sun telling us it has to happen.

If you move out of the dream of the planet, you will completely shift your assemblage point to the point of view of your soul. First, from the back of the soul, you will see who faces the dream. Then you will shift to the other side of the soul and see who sees the spirit. This is a big jump from one part of the soul to the other.

To make the shift, a part of our reason perceives the black light of unconditional love which goes directly to the soul, opens it, and lets the spirit flow out. The spirit aligns with that part of reason which recognizes unconditional love. Together, they can do everything. They clean the mind completely and they express their understanding to the outside. This is the Christ, the Buddha part of the reason that is in complete alignment with the spirit.

In the energetic system we know as reality, reason is the king. We have the Judge and the Victim. In the Toltec idealized energetic system, spirit is the king. The only element of reason that persists in the spiritual energetic system is that part which reflects the soul.

The size of the soul is microscopic at first, but it is connected with every cell in your body. The soul is deep in the human egg. It is in the nucleus of the will, in the bubble of perception. The spirit is a little piece of the sun trapped in matter. Our DNA is in direct connection with the spirit. What we are is spirit. What we are is God. Our will encircles our human egg and it lasts until our death.

When you have a choice of two roads to go down, choose both for a while. Soon one of the paths will not feel right. It does not matter if you make a mistake. Try to love yourself for trying. Say to yourself, "I love you for trying even though it blew up in your face."

After a while you get better and better at feeling. It is like a muscle you haven't used before. You will say to yourself, "Oh boy, I had a feeling that was going to go wrong, but I did it anyway." If you do that five times you are going to think, "Wait a second. I've had this feeling before but I did not pay attention." You will start to let go of reason and trust your feelings as you react to your environment. It is a way of living life.

Second Attention: Beyond the Nightmare

Miguel Ruiz:

The dream of life is a synonym for our whole reality. The dream of life that we are presently living reflects who we believe we are and what we believe about everything in our reality. This dream is the result of what we have learned from our ability to perceive. We have created our reality, our entire dream, and our mind by learning all that we believe through our perceptions.

Because we are multidimensional living beings, we can perceive thousands of things at the same time. Yet, one of the magical parts of being human is that we have the ability to discriminate. We can screen out all the perceptions we do not choose to notice and focus on the perception that we want to study. This power to choose one perception among millions of possible stimuli and to focus upon it is what we call "attention."

Attention allows us to focus our perception on what we want to learn. In order to learn to walk, to ride a bicycle, or to play a piano, we must, in the beginning, focus our attention and repeatedly practice until the action becomes automatic. Then the knowledge of the action becomes part of us.

We use attention to learn everything that we know and everything that we believe.

We use attention for the first time to create our reality, to create our dream. The result of our using the first attention, or the attention for the first time, is the creation of this nightmare that we call hell.

The tool that we can use to transform the dream is the same tool that we used to create this dream in the first place — our attention.

When we review all that we know and think to be true in an effort to decide whether or not we believe it, we are using attention for the second time in the process we call the inventory. Using our attention for the second time changes the dream. Exercising our second attention removes limitations that formerly bound us, and it expands our consciousness. Eventually we will discover that we are dreaming a new dream, a dream of life where everything is possible, a dream that buoys our self-confidence, our hopes and expectations. The new dream we call heaven on earth.

Through second attention, our dream can carry us wherever and whenever we want to be. We become explorers. We are no longer dogmatic about anything. We have a wide view of the whole universe. What was not known becomes known, but something always remains unknowable, in the nagual of total spirit. Second attention gives us control over the dream and the awareness that we are becoming God.

Miguel was in the state of second attention when he learned from the Book of Hermes and when he met Jesus and the Buddha. To those in second attention, all is alive and available all the time.

Stalking Your Own Dream

Miguel Ruiz:

As a stalker, you will design your own dream. I am designing my life. It is a lot of work, but I love every step of the way. I try to put myself in everything I do. When you are conscious of the power in your every action, you are transmitting love. However, it is still possible to feel a wound, and if this occurs, another inventory may be needed to cleanse all wounds.

If you are in a state of love, you have nothing to lose. You are in a state of oneness. You are God on earth.

This is a beautiful concept. Once you awaken, it ceases to be an abstract concept and becomes truth. This is what you are. But, until you are awake, it is just a concept. You will still have the poison inside. You will still feel personal importance. These are the traps of the old dream. The dream will not let you go because it cannot handle love.

It is wonderful to have knowledge, but knowledge is also a trap unless the knowledge is activated. Millions of souls are trapped because they do not know what love is. They think they do, but they know about love only according to the dream which traps everyone. To awaken from the dream, one must become a stalker.

Everyone, at a certain level, is a stalker. Stalking is the only way we make something come true. For most people, stalking is just a way of survival. For a warrior, stalking is a way to escape. For a master, stalking is an art. We need to become artists of stalking. If we are already warriors, we are using stalking to change our dream of the planet. This effort is an interior "war" between the old illusion of hell and the new dream of heaven on earth. We use stalking to create art and to create beauty, which are the qualities of heaven.

The art of stalking is the result of years of training. You reach mastery the moment that you gain awareness that everything you do and everything you say is an act of power. As a corollary of this awareness, you then accept responsibility for everything you do and for everything you say. You will consciously direct that power to create the new dream of heaven on earth.

CHAPTER EIGHT

THE WORLD OF JUSTICE

In december 1992, Miguel went on a journey to Teotihuacán expecting to be profoundly changed when he returned. His inner guidance told him his trip to Teotihuacán would be more dangerous than any he had made previously. He had made the decision to climb to the top of the Pyramid of the Sun and shamanically "jump into the sun" by surrendering his life force to the pure spirit of light. The act of power he contemplated would help him achieve a much higher level of awareness, but such a self-actuated trial could have fatal results for a master shaman who is able to shut down his breathing and pulse by an act of will. Ancient Toltecs used this act of power to ascend out of their bodies. Should he survive, Miguel knew he would be permanently altered by the ordeal. He risked losing his identity, just as he had when he gave up the practice of medicine.

Miguel survived the ordeal, but his expectation of change was realized so dynamically that those who accompanied him felt he was no longer the same person who had started the trip with them. In appearance he had the same body and the same expressions, but they knew the person he had been was gone forever.

Since that time Miguel's appearance and his personality have transformed. The new Miguel is a world teacher who travels and lectures to an ever-widening audience, yet within himself his perception of his role has become one of detachment.

Prior to his transformation, Miguel had believed his special destiny was to impart Toltec wisdom to anyone who sought it. He had dedicated his whole life to carrying out that mission. Today, he says:

Miguel Ruiz:

Everything was gone. There was no mission. There was no man. There was no life. Inside I felt completely full of joy, peace, and love, just to be. I no longer have to justify anything to myself or to anyone else. The meaning of my work has changed. I no longer feel that I have a special gift to give others. I had thought I was God's worker, and that he sent me for a reason. That is not truth anymore for me.

Intellectually, I hardly think at all now. Sometimes I read, but I have hardly any activity in the mind.

It is like a state of Samadhi. After this single day, I see the world with a different perception. I see it without judgment. The result is amazing. I'm not worried about the planet at all. I do not worry about nature. I do not worry about other people, war, a tornado, or someone shooting at me. I know that whatever happens has to happen. It is done as it should be and I trust it one hundred percent.

I see a world with justice. We are already in a world of justice. We have searched for it for thousands of years. From this new state of mind, I can see all the nightmares we have created in this world. It is easy to understand that emotional and physical suffering of humans comes from what we have created ourselves.

After that day, I could see myself again at two years old, playing all the time and having fun. I couldn't see the world of injustice yet. I didn't know that the way humans dream is a nightmare.

True bliss is to know without the innocence of childhood this is a world of justice. We cannot remove the nightmare if we remain innocent as children. Children who are too innocent are like lambs. We must introduce them to hell so they can get out of hell as soon as possible.

Miguel entered a state of radical trust during that fateful journey. When he teaches now, he speaks from an assurance that he can trust whatever comes through him.

Miguel Ruiz:

I don't have to rethink what I know. I have no doubts now about whether my words are accurate. It is not important. I have found out something very interesting about truth. Truth is individual. What is true for me may not be true for anyone else.

Each listener at a lecture absorbs what I am saying differently. Each one wants to hear some of the message but not all. Each believes in a certain way. I expose what I know. I no longer ask for feedback. I ask for questions only to clarify the way they believe.

I used to teach "avoid judgment," but I found I still judged myself. After that day, I surrendered that. I no longer judge myself. I honor myself just the way I am.

I used to have to express what I am. But there is no need. It is more important to observe what others want to hear. I have not changed my talks, but I have changed my method of observation.

I know that nobody really needs me, including my two sons, my mother, my wife, and my students. Once you see a world of justice, you can be yourself one hundred percent. You find you have a strong communication with everybody. You are completely open to what you are and you see that everyone else is you. It makes you closer to other people. The sense of need is what causes rejection of other people. Once you know that no one needs you, you have no rejection or fear of anyone.

This is almost like flying out of the body. If you can become needless yourself, you can be there for everybody.

Respect others.

Respect their right to make their own choices.

Remember that you can choose to do something or not, with kindness. You do not have to do anything if you do not want to.

I learned to respect everything just the way it is. I no longer see problems. The injustice people feel in the world is an illusion. Injustice does not come from outside. It comes from the decisions each of us makes throughout our life. Those in society who seem to be victims of injustice put themselves into their situations through choices they have made. No one else is responsible for all the poison in their dream. It is their own hell. Why does the dream have to control them? They have chosen to dream this. The disease we call hell can be healed.

I used to pray. I felt sorry for them. How they suffer! How they need! But we find we have built a society based on need. Outside of the dream, there is no fear and no need.

There is a different way to see the world and it is much more beautiful. When you give up need, you are not afraid to be hurt. You have no expectations. You have no need for boundaries. You merge with everything. You don't think. You feel bliss, but not innocence. You have to get beyond innocence with wisdom, not just knowledge. Without need, you are wise.

The body dies and the brain dies, but the mind lives on after death and it feels as though it is still alive. The brain needs sugar and oxygen to survive, but the mind does not. After death, it takes time before the mind finally notices it is dead. The function of the mind is to dream. Even in a sleeping dream, you feel as if you have a body and you can talk, and sometimes you notice that you are dreaming. Your reason will try to wake you up. Reason ceases to function at death, and therefore nothing tells you are dead.

It is an act of justice to die. If you want to experience life, you have to take risks all the time. If you are so afraid to die, you are not really alive.

To know the joys of living each moment fully, moment by moment, we must accept that death can claim us whenever it wishes. Death is the natural corrollary of life, a part of the natural continuum in which energy realizes itself. The detachment that comes from accepting death does not imply sterility or coldness. On the contrary, once the desperation of holding on is relinquished everything can be savored in the moment.

When a person has a terminal illness, if there is a known cure, then I advise taking advantage of it. If there is none, I do not advise medical procedures that prolong suffering.

The mind does not want to die, so it lets the body suffer needlessly. It would be more just to let it die.

When a person you are concerned about is near death or suffering from illness, if you feel sorry for her, you are not helping at all. You can be a more effective healer if you remain needless and detached, yet loving, accepting the way it is. This is justice.

CHAPTER NINE

LIFE AFTER DEATH

When Miguel gives lectures, he begins with a prayer to our Father, Creator of the Universe. He asks that the Creator use his voice, his eyes, his hands, and his heart to share Himself with all His children. In this chapter, taken from his lectures, he focuses on the subject of life after death.

Miguel Ruiz:

Death is nothing but a transformation. It is merely a concept that scares humans when they face any transformation. Fear of death is often especially strong when the human body begins to lose awareness at the end of life. The body ceases to feel or to breathe. The body is aware that it will be destroyed, while, little by little, we return to God. Nonetheless, we speak of life after death, which means we believe we will still be alive after the body dies.

For thousands of years, men have asked themselves about life after death. Their answers have ranged from "Everything stops" to "We will live again through reincarnation."

There is life after death although we cannot prove it. We cannot prove many things that we believe, but we know they exist.

The human body needs material energy to survive, in the form of water, food, and oxygen. Dreams, emotions, and the mind do not require material energy, so why should they be destroyed?

Our mind is alive. The mind is made from ethereal energy. The mind is made by thinking. We think with the mind, not the brain. The mind has awareness.

The brain is a tool of perception. With the brain, we can perceive light and sounds that are transformed by the brain into ethereal energy.

Whatever we perceive has an emotional component. The emotional component will create the energy of the emotions, the imagination, the astral mind, and the dream. The main function of the brain is to transform energy from matter into ethereal energy. This wonderful process converts oxygen and sugar into emotion.

The function of the mind is to dream twenty-four hours a day. The waking dream has a material structure. In sleep, the dream also seems to have a structure. While awake, our mind is affected by cycles of energy through the day as the light changes, and this rhythm gives the mind a notion of time and space. During sleep, we do not perceive energy from outside ourselves, but the mind dreams images including an image of our own body. We can talk, see, and even fly in a dream. We do not notice that we are asleep when we are dreaming.

The two different kinds of dream flow into one another. The sleeping dream continues the waking dream without the structure of time and space, and vice versa. We can dream our whole life in an hour, or, in an hour, we can live five or ten minutes.

Something makes the connection between the inner dream and the outer dream. That something is reason. Reason is the part of the mind that tries to qualify and understand everything. Reason wants to say, this is real and this is unreal. Reason gives us the illusion that the dream is real as long as the dream has a material framework. We see the material framework as reality. We do not notice that we are interpreting reality according to the dream we are in at the moment.

In our interpretation of the dream, we make our own movie. We will find that our interpretation is no different from that of others who witnessed the same interaction, so that tells us that we are all dreaming together.

The mind is alive. You might think, "I am the body," or "I am the mind," and then your mind will be afraid to die. It is afraid that when the body and brain die, life will be over and it will have no further awareness, but that is not true.

I had a car accident when I was in medical school. The car crashed and was completely destroyed. I saw myself asleep at the wheel. At that moment I was out of my body so I knew that I am not my body.

I was completely shaken because what I had thought was real was not real. I knew I was living an illusion. I had many goals at that time. I was at the university with only one year left before becoming a medical doctor. I was worried that I was leaving reality, but it was not real at all. My concept of reality changed immediately. That was the moment I knew that we are not finished when the body dies. We continue.

After the accident, I began to study my dreams because I think what happens to us when we die is like a dream. I started with the notion that the state of death will be very similar to what happens when we dream. That is exactly true. The body dies and the mind continues to dream.

When we go to sleep and we dream, our brain is completely shut off. Our reason notices that we are dreaming and it tries to wake the brain. Reason's task is to say, "this is real; this is not real." Reason always needs to hook into a material framework. The material framework makes the reason feel safe. Without it, the reason has no support.

In the death state, this interaction between the reason and the brain cannot occur. Without the body, reason cannot awaken the brain and make the connection with the material framework; yet, the mind, without the brain, continues to dream.

The mind retains all our identity and memory. It keeps going even if the supply of energy is cut. The mind is not receiving any new emotional energy from the dead brain, but it is still attached to its memories. The mind can suddenly become aware of its death state, and that may be a shock.

Many die without awareness of their death. Many who are living in their own body do not have the awareness that they are dead. Those who remain in the dream of hell are actually dead, in the point of view of the Toltecs.

We remember that everything that exists is God. In the dream of hell we dream we are not God. We have created a God who is superior to us. The God we have created takes away our responsibility to be what we are, and metes out both fear and punishment.

The day the dreamer awakes and becomes God is the same as resurrection. First, we have to become aware that we are dead. Then we can awake.

Miguel discovered that the ancient Toltecs knew that the mind would continue to dream after death. They worried that they would die and the nightmare would continue, but they were not sure how long the nightmare would last. They focused their efforts on how to control the dream while they were alive, both the waking and sleeping dream. This was the knowledge they taught. Essentially, they discovered that everything the mind perceives is a dream.

The Toltecs learned that the mind is not eternal. The mind will eventually die and go back to the spirit, or to the intent, but the mind continues to dream and be transformed for many years after the brain dies. When the mind finally dies, that is the end of the dream. This interval in which the mind continues to dream explains many paranormal phenomena that happen in this world. Once we understand the death process, we will realize why people hear ghosts and see objects moving apparently by their own power.

Miguel Ruiz:

Dying means the liberation of the body, and it entails losing the connection, or losing the reason. The result of death is that the dream is split in two. The mind continues to dream the inner dream, but it is no longer connected with the outer dream. Even though the body might still be functioning, though decomposing, the mind loses its rational connection.

The body is a human being, and the mind is also a human being. They mix and are connected by the reason. At death, the mind takes responsibility for itself.

Fundamentally, we are living an illusion. The happiness we seek is illusory, too. It is a ghost. We may feel happiness for a brief moment but it is not sustained because happiness is not from outside. Happiness is a state of mind like suffering. It can only come in our personal dream, not from material reality. Our success and happiness depend upon the quality of our personal dream in ethereal reality. If we are dreaming the nightmare when we die, we will continue to do so until we discover that we are dead. This is very similar to discovering we are asleep in the midst of a nightmare.

There will be a moment after death that we grasp, "Oh, I am dead. I have no body. I have no brain. All those goals I had are gone and I am helpless, because my own creations—my own fears, my own anger—are hurting me." At that moment, no one else will be interacting with us that we are aware of until we discover how to control and change the dream.

The possibility of changing the dream after we die is very low, partially because the mind will eventually be absorbed. The dream will fade, little by little, until our inner energy that made our dream is absorbed and the nightmare is over. Then we receive a new body, a new brain, new parents, a new name, in a different environment—and the new cycle begins.

The process will continue, life after life, until in one of those lives we decide that this is a dream. Everything around us is a dream within a material framework. With that awareness, we again have the opportunity to change the nightmare into a pleasant dream.

At this moment, you are alive. Your opportunity to change the dream is excellent. You have only to become aware that you are dreaming and so is everyone else around you. That single perception alters the way you interact with other people. You see that they are dreaming, but your dream has changed and it continues to change more and more as your awareness grows. We see that we are dreaming with our minds, not with our body nor with our brain, and we sense that the mind will continue to dream beyond death. Death loses power when we accept that what dies is the dream, not the dreamer. We are what continues.

Behind the dream lies the mind, and behind the mind lies energy. All energy has awareness, perception, and memory. We can perceive energy without ears or eyes. All energy is alive.

This is the point. If we can perceive energy without benefit of our physical self then we are close to the source of creation. According to both science and religion, the source of creation is energy. Energy and God seem to be exactly the same, but this is not precisely true.

Energy is the result of the will, the result of intent. In the Bible, we read that it was dark and the first thing God created was the light. From that, he created everything else.

Everything is created from energy, from light, including ourselves. We are light. The dream is light. The dreamer is light. The soul is light. Energy is light.

All action and reaction begins in the spirit. Spirit is that property of energy that makes any transformation possible. Spirit is the pure consciousness that creates everything. It is light by itself. It is eternal. It cannot be destroyed.

Therefore, if we are light and light is eternal, death does not exist. Death is a state of illusion and it only exists in a dream. We find now that the creation of the universe is nothing but a dream, a dream of intent, a dream of spirit, a dream of God.

If God awakes, everything disappears. He is the Supreme Dreamer. He is everywhere because everything is energy and energy transforms at every moment.

Why be afraid of death when we have this awareness? The body is nothing but an edifice of God's intent. An edifice of light is light. We are not the brain. We are not the heart. We are what makes our heart beat. We are light. We are life. Life uses all these instruments to perceive, to transform, to express, to live, and to die.

When the body dies, we will continue to perceive with different tools. The mind dies and we still will perceive, even without tools because we are light. This is what Jesus meant when he said, "I am the light. I am he who gives life because I am eternal."

This is the Toltec message, too. There is only one message, because there is just One, in all realities, in all universes. If we understand that, we can understand everything.

If we focus our intention, we will understand it.

Miguel reminds us that in the Bible, Jesus told us "I die daily," which is in accord with the Toltec concept that there is only transformation.

Miguel Ruiz:

Death is transformation and it occurs constantly. Every moment that has passed is death. Each moment gives us the opportunity to live in the present. The past does not exist. The future has not yet come. I am dying all the time. I am adapting to every change in the dream of life. I die every day because I am not attached to what happened a moment ago. I let it go, and this makes me free. That is what we call the Toltec way, surrender to death.

When we surrender to death, we live only in the moment. Many people who do not surrender to death live in the past or the future, and thereby they miss the present. In the point of view of the Toltecs, they are dead. The resurrection Jesus offered everyone was that you can live now and not be trapped by the difficulties of the past.

The Angel of Death

Miguel Ruiz:

There is an Angel of Death and an Angel of Life who teach us how to live intensely every second of our lives. The Angel of Death clears away the debris of our lives.

Try to imagine, Miguel says with a smile, that you have in your home all of your past lovers. What are you going to do with them? The Angel of Death takes them away so you can experience whoever is coming into your life.

Imagine as well that everything you ever owned was stored in your home, even the toys you had in childhood and every discarded object you have ever had. With the concept of the Angel of Death, you know that nothing really belongs to you. It all belongs to the Angel of Death. Whatever comes to us, we can use and enjoy, but we do not own it. If we lose something, we will suffer less if we realize that we never really owned it anyway. Traveling light, without the pressure of ownership and responsibility, makes us ready for happiness at any moment.

Jesus brought the silent knowledge to the world two thousand years ago, but we are only now learning that we do not have to age. If we die every moment, we can transform our body. Time stops. Space stops. We can be many places at once.

Miguel Ruiz:

Everything has a reason for being, including the cycle of life in a human body. We have the opportunity to really enjoy this universe while we are living. The idea that we will live forever in this universe limits our experience of other universes that may be as beautiful as this one. Death, the transformation of this life state into another form, is a process that is working perfectly. There is no reason to change it. Once you lose attachment for the body, you are ready to leave it at any time. We can love the body, respect the body, and honor the body without being attached to it or identifying with it.

Living every moment as though it were your last chance to enjoy this universe adds zest to living. You can put into every action the consideration that the action is between life and death.

The concept of the Angel of Death helps you to control the dream when you are awake. By making a friend of the Angel of Death, you can lose the biggest of human fears. Once you have nothing to lose, everything changes. We can live for the pleasure of living.

Each day can give us supreme pleasure if we put our awareness into our breath. We can enjoy each of our actions in the dream, and realize that they are being absorbed by the Angel of Death who is constantly behind us absorbing each moment. That awareness is love.

Your life can be a constant meditation. There is formal meditation, which we will discuss in the next chapter, but there is also informal meditation that can be carried out in all circumstances.

The Way to Meditate

Miguel Ruiz:

You can meditate with eyes closed or open. Contemplation is a way of meditation. You are alive. You can be in a state of bliss. You can teach others to meditate and to reach this state. This will help them to shift their awareness and to create a pleasant dream in place of their nightmare.

In meditation, the first step is to separate the mind from the other organs of the body.

In the second step, you go into your mind, the soul, and the spirit in ever higher levels of meditation.

One of the by-products of meditation is the breakup of the dream and the release of intent. Intent can make miracles.

Meditation becomes a way of life. It is a prayer. It is one of the greatest methods for cleaning the mind; not the only method, but it is one of the most powerful and easiest.

Meditation also gives you control and awareness on the level of the ego. When you create a beautiful dream in a state of blissful meditation, your eyes change and you begin to perceive love from everything. There will be a love interaction between you and your action. In pure meditation, you can be awake and expressing yourself in the world with eyes of love. Love perceives love. This is heaven on earth, the transformation that does not wait for death. It can happen here, in life, by our intent.

Meditation While Eating

It is not important what you put in your mouth. You can be a vegetarian or a meat eater and still conduct a meditative life.

Pick up the food you are going to eat. Put it into your mouth. Close your eyes. Chew your food very well. Use your tongue to perceive all the flavors. Feel each flavor. It will be like hearing each instrument in an orchestra when you listen to music. Each flavor is alive. Eating gives you so much pleasure, it is like a supreme act of love. Everything you eat will be modified by your love. This is a ritual approach to eating with awareness. With just a small amount of food, you will be satisfied. It adds to your pleasure to hum a little as you eat and it strengthens your connection with food.

You can apply this same meditative approach to many other parts of your day, such as taking a shower. We benefit when we enjoy living in our body and we take good care of our body.

A Witness to Miguel's Near-Death Experience

by David Dibble

David Dibble is a student, associate, and friend of Miguel's who is a master teacher specializing in transforming business by means of the Toltec Silent Knowledge and Total Quality principles. On a journey to Hawaii with Miguel, he witnessed Miguel's brush with death in the summer of 1994, which he describes in this story:

David Dibble:

Miguel was taking a group of his students to Hawaii on a journey to some of the power points that dot the Hawaiian Islands. My wife, Linda, and I very much wanted to go with him, knowing it would be a powerful learning experience. However, we didn't have the time or the money. Because I was working long hours, Linda wondered if she should make the trip alone. She decided to do the thing that had always worked best in the past. She asked Miguel what he thought. As usual, we got an answer we didn't expect. Miguel was of the opinion that both of us should go with him. I had learned that when Miguel recommends an action, it's usually best to heed his words. With many reservations, we chose to damn the torpedoes, and donned our flowered shirts and sandals. What a trip this would turn out to be.

One of the power points we were scheduled to visit on Maui is the Haleakala volcano, which has the largest inactive crater in the world—over twenty miles in circumference and three thousand feet deep. The rim of the crater, which is nearly always obscured from below by impressive white clouds, is over ten thousand feet above the crystal clear Hawaiian water. Looking into the crater from the rim, I was reminded of a moon-scape—black, jagged, and without life. I felt a whisper of apprehension as we started down the dark lava trail that zigzagged its way for over five miles into this foreboding womb of the world.

We made our way to the bottom of the main crater and found another small crater, approximately eighty feet deep with a very steep trail falling into the pit. Miguel asked me if I thought we should go into the crater and, with uncharacteristic caution, the words popped out of my mouth, "No, Miguel, I don't think we should go down there." Miguel walked to the trail and started down. I took a couple of deep breaths and followed suit. The trail was not only steep, it was made of sand-like crushed lava that was deep and tended to slide in mini-avalanches with each step. I knew it would be difficult walking up this path where everything seemed to be pulled into the abyss. I even remarked to Miguel that this place reminded me of an Ant Lion pit and we were the ants. A few other students joined us and we began a ceremony.

The ceremony ended rather abruptly when Miguel said it was time to go. A few members of the group began to look for small rocks that they might take with them.

Miguel started up the trail and then turned and said to me, "Get the others. We must go now." He began laboring his way up the trail and I returned to gather up the others.

After an exhausting climb in the stifling heat, I found Miguel lying on a large rock at the top of the small crater. He motioned me over and indicated that he wanted to tell me something in confidence. I knew that something was wrong. All the color had gone from his face and he was gasping for breath. What he said next chilled me to my core.

Miguel softly whispered these words. "David, you must not be scared. I am having a heart attack. I have severe pains in my chest and in my left arm. I must leave this place or I will die. You must not tell the others because they will be afraid. If I can get back to Gaya, she will be able to help me. I have tried to heal myself, but I do not have the energy in this place. We must leave this place."

A wave of fear swept through my body as I realized what he was saying. I asked him what he wanted me to do. He said that I should help him walk out of the crater when he had regained some of his strength. "Although we might not make it, we must try." We embarked on the most incredible five-mile walk of my life.

Most of the rest of our group had gone ahead and were not aware of our travails. Five women and I were the only ones left to assist the master in the event he became too weak to walk. It didn't take the women long to catch onto the fact that Miguel was very sick. He had to stop, sit down, and rest after every laborious one hundred paces or so.

Each time Miguel could go no further, the women would gather around him, hold his hands or feet, send him their love and energy, and pray for his life. I would pull energy from the sun and direct it into Miguel's heart.

About half way up the trail, Miguel stopped, sat down, and gazed into the nothingness of the blackened crater. He was as white as the clouds that drifted slowly through the blue Hawaiian sky. He was cold, sweaty, and clammy, all at the same time. His breath was shallow and irregular. My teacher was dying. When I looked into his eyes, I experienced something that changed my life forever. I felt his ecstasy. I felt his bliss and love. My fear of death, both his and mine, vanished. I sat in bliss with Miguel and five beautiful women who had become living angels. Through shimmering and grateful eyes, I perceived only love where there had been fear and desolation. The color began to come back into Miguel's face.

We started walking again and I felt compelled to "push" Miguel out of the crater. I held one hand to the sun and placed the other in the small of Miguel's back. I told him to lean into my hand and let me push him up the trail. The walking suddenly became less arduous for Miguel's body and heart. As we neared the rim of the crater, Miguel's energy seemed to be growing stronger. He related a final request. He would not, under any circumstances, allow us to take him to the hospital. Although Miguel had been a medical doctor and a surgeon in Mexico, he knew he could heal himself much faster through the proper use of energy than anything that could be done at the hospital. Within two weeks of his heart attack, Miguel had completely healed himself.

My teacher has shown me that there is nothing to fear about death of the human body. In the dream of the planet, there is birth, death, and "life" is the hell that is experienced in between. In the old dream, encapsulated in a context of fear, being born is always a sentence of death and despair. Outside of the dream, there is only eternal love, a love so exquisitely complete that it is the other name for God. It is also the other name for you, your real name.

Gaya's Vision
During Miguel's Heart Attack

We are all eggs. I have discovered that the process of reproduction is the same throughout the universe. Everything is in a constant state of reproduction, as above, so below. The universe is an egg filled with every kind of energy that exists in this dream we call life.

In Hawaii, while Miguel had a heart attack in the crater, I was up above on the trail. My uterus went into spasm and I collapsed onto a rock. Across from me, I saw a trough in the rocks. I looked up at the sun and felt a force of energy pass through me, up that trough, and into the sky. I birthed all of this energy . . . out there. I birthed an egg of energy for Miguel.

When We Are Dead We Have Wings

When we are dead
We are like the snake
Slithering in the dust,
The dust of emotional pain.

But when we awake
The wings of our Divinity unfold
And we become the feathered serpent
Who flies to heaven —
Quetzalcoatl.

~ MIGUEL ANGEL RUIZ

CHAPTER TEN

THE WAY OF DEATH
AT TEOTIHUACÁN

Miguel Ruiz:

I had a dream in the Plaza of the Temple of Quetzalcoatl on one of my early trips to Teotihuacán. The apprentices who had come with me were busy carrying out a ritual I had directed for them. I sat alone on the "Island of Hell" which is in the middle of the plaza.

In my dream, I was with old men who often were in my dreams. They were skinny, white-haired Indians from India. I saw a man who was in the process of dying. He was with me. He was one of the guides of my dreams. His teacher was helping him to die.

The teacher had a dual vision of here and the place of after death. I heard the teacher explain time and the Angel of Death. The teacher pointed out to the man that his only way to transcend was to totally surrender to the Angel of Death. The only reason he would suffer is because he resisted the Angel of Death.

This is true for all of us. We suffer when we are afraid of losing what we are and what we have.

The teacher said to me, "The time is coming. This is the last time you will be here in a human body. Still, you must accomplish all you have left to do in your dream of life. The Angel of Death will return at the exact moment to take you to meet your destiny, but she will bring you a messenger and it will be someone like you who has surrendered completely and entered Paradise to eat the fruit of eternity. It will be like a marriage with your Creator. From the moment you eat the fruit, your eyes will see only beauty and will experience only the feeling of love."

The Angel of Death came with another human, who was a smiling woman in a state of ecstacy. The Angel of Death brought her in silence and left her. The teacher said, "The Angel of Death did not come to take you. She will return very soon. You will become like the messenger."

To see this woman, radiant with happiness and joy and love for everything makes you want to die right away, but the Angel of Death says to enjoy your life, enjoy your agony, and enjoy your death.

I saw a strong man sitting in a chair with a sword in his hand. Behind him was a portal with a spiral of light in it. I could see the night and the stars. In the center of the spiral was a sacred, powerful rock and on the rock I saw the Tree of Eternity.

The warrior sitting there guards the portal. He carries the sword of justice and truth. He cuts the remains of whatever is not love from whomever passes him. The sword is the last purification.

I believe this figure is that of Archangel Ariel. The spiral is the same symbol as the Garden of Eden.

My message was, "Your time is short. You have had enough time to surrender. Let everyone you love know that you love them. You may never return, but they do not need to worry. You will be in a state of happiness.

"At the moment of death, the Angel of Death's eyes will penetrate yours completely. She will give you a moment or two to surrender. Then she will walk toward you and your body will be dead, but you will be aware of her eyes. You will feel the jolt, but you will be happy and ecstatic."

The Angel of Death did exactly as the teacher said. The angel did turn and look with a beautiful smile. As she took one step toward me, a burden was lifted. As soon as she was in front of me, she said, "Come with me. It is your time. I am going to take you to your wedding."

She took me to the warrior. He said, "This is the moment of your awakening, your resurrection. You are coming to life again. You were living in a nightmare and now you are aware of who you really are."

He swung the sword over my back and then forward. He said, "Go and accomplish your destiny. It is your wedding day."

I floated over the spiral to the tree. Then I was married with the spirit of God. That spiral for me is the double-headed snake.

Knowing that dream, I have no fear of death. As a warrior, long before your body dies, you start reaching that place of happiness from surrendering to death. We die all the time, with every loss. Death is an illusion. Live always in the present. That is eternity.

Our fear of death is an illusion. Whatever is lost brings the new. If we resist loss, we are dead. We are in the past, not the present. We suffer because we fear to let go. We have eyes only for injustice. When we surrender, we have the joy to explore. Not knowing what to expect is happiness.

From my dream, I learned what information is stored in the rocks of Teotihuacán. The vision came from the communion I had with the rocks. I am sure that I am not the only one to have had that vision.

My vision clarified why the builders of Teotihuacán chose the structures they did. Suddenly, the plan of the place seemed to make sense. That place symbolized the whole dream of humanity. Our attachments are the same, all around the world.

I had a teacher while I was practicing medicine at a clinic in the desert. He opened me to this sort of dream. He taught me that I am just a vibration. I can take on the vibration of the rocks or other people. My student apprentices try to take on my vibration.

Knowing that the Angel of Death is taking you to bliss, you want to hurry to die, but when you learn to reach heaven here on earth, you are not in a hurry. When you marry God, you are in a state of eternal honeymoon. Even breathing is a joy when it becomes conscious. How can anyone be unhappy when he experiences the pleasure of breathing sixteen times a minute? Just being you is to be eternal when you live in the present.

If you are in hell, all you can give is hell. You cannot love anyone else until you love yourself first. To be happy, don't judge yourself. Perfection is already here.

I. The Temple of Quetzalcoatl

As you begin your journey to the Pyramid of Quetzalcoatl, Miguel advises you should read about the place and then visit it mentally. Lawrence Andrews (*Magical Blend*, issue 47, 1995, page 25) recaptures his journey with Miguel along the "Path of Freedom" that begins at the Citadel of Quetzalcoatl where "the Mastery of Awareness was taught through dance and drama."

The Plaza of the Temple of Quetzalcoatl is the symbolic head of a snake facing the Pyramid of Quetzalcoatl that rises behind the temple. The steps leading up to the temple can be seen as its open mouth. This temple complex is dedicated to the Feathered Serpent and the Planet Venus, the Goddess of Love.

Throughout Mesoamerica, Greece, Egypt, and Rome, Venus is the Goddess of Love. She is the morning and evening star, depending upon the time of year. Teotihuacános once measured time by coordinating the cyclical movements of Venus with those of the earth and the moon.

Miguel has discerned, between the temple and the pyramid of Quetzalcoatl, a line that separates the human from the Divine. When you are in the plaza of this complex, you cannot see the pyramid, but from the top of the temple that stands in front (if you were allowed to climb the steps leading up to it), you suddenly see the pyramid looming up and you receive a physical sensation of awe from seeing it.

The pyramid is built in platforms upon whose frontal faces carved heads of the Feathered Serpent, the jaguar, and the pop-eyed rain god Tlaloc are mounted. A pattern of waves and seashells identifies the place with water and the serpent. Its surface is made of larger rocks in mortar, surrounded by lines of smaller stones that form a graphic design. This style prevails throughout the site at Teotihuacán.

The very rocks themselves seem to reflect the love these structures signify. This love is superior to human love. Miguel describes it as the Christ in the Rocks. He feels a sensation of totally identifying with the low vibration of energy that remains in the rocks through the centuries of time that have passed since Teotihuacán was built.

Miguel Ruiz:

The Pyramid of Quetzalcoatl represents the spirit of God. The open area of the plaza represents the human mind. Hell only exists in the human mind. It is an illusion, based on fear. In hell there is only injustice. Hell is experienced as the emotional poison of anger, envy, and greed.

Neither your body nor your soul has a hell. They respond to what is in the mind. If you have the eyes of anger or sadness it will distort your view. Eyes of love make everything beautiful. Our eyes are dominated by the way we judge.

Your first task along the Avenue of the Dead is to forego judging as much as you possibly can, and to exorcize the Victim within your mind.

A small pyramid, a platform-like low temple, stands in front of the main temple. On maps this is called the Citadel, but to Miguel it is the Island of Hell in the Ocean of Hell. The ocean contains all fears of the unknown and our fears are our dream of hell. Our dream forms the inside movies we carry around with us. We are the producer, director, and chief actor in these fear-laden films.

Miguel Ruiz:

On the Island of Hell, we have the illusion of being safe. It is a place in the mind where we hoard all that belongs to us. We think, "This is my family, my house, my money, my car, my career, my accomplishments," and we feel safer as we make this island bigger and bigger with more and more attachments to what is ours. But, the island is ruled by a fear of loss of anything we cherish.

We envy the islands of others, not realizing that they are trapped in hell in their safety zones. Each of us is trapped by the illusions we have amassed on our islands.

There is only one way to escape from the Island of Hell and that is to cross the Ocean of Hell and reach the snake on the stairs of the Temple of Quetzalcoatl. This temple is the exit from hell. It is the only place on the site where evil—also an illusion—exists. Small temples are placed on all sides of the plaza. The pyramid itself protects the east. The temples surrounding its plaza are the guardians who contain the evil generated by our nightmares.

It takes an act of courage to let go and face fear. This is true in all the traditions of the world. Demons on the outside of Christian churches represent the fears we leave behind as we enter the sanctuary. In fairy tales, the hero must conquer a demon or dragon to reach a happy ending. To reach bliss, we have to surrender to the Angel of Death and the illusions of what we think we are. Our illusions make our hell.

Hell is the Place of the Ghosts. Only ghosts live there. Ghosts have the sensation of being alive. To live in hell is to be a ghost. Paradoxically, we have to die to our former life in order to escape from hell. Dying leads us to clarity. We will recognize that what we have believed to be real was an illusion. This is similar to the Indian concept of Maya.

Each person has the task of creating a private and sacred place that is beyond hell and beyond the fears inculcated by society, religion, and the domestication process in the family. In the coming years, Miguel prophesies that this will be done by individuals without the intercessor of any priest or church. His teaching is a preparation for the time that is coming when human beings must create their own route to God.

After they visit Teotihuacán, Miguel takes his student groups to a church and relates it to visiting the temple of Quetzalcoatl. People go to church and face the altar, looking for God. They want to escape from the hell of their sins and their wounds. They may succeed in releasing some of their emotional poison, but they rarely find release from fear because today's religions are systems that breed fear. In one sense, our religions accept the idea that this is a place of hell. We can see this in the prevalent belief that heaven is elsewhere in a state of off-planet freedom from judgment and peace. Temporal punishment on earth and threatened eternal punishment make heaven seem unobtainable to all but the few.

Miguel Ruiz:

The ruler of hell is fear. One of the big demons in hell is the Judge. Another is the Victim. But, the greatest demon is our belief system, which is what rules the way we dream.

We find ourselves on the Island of Hell because we are afraid to let go of our attachments. The Island of Hell is in the Plaza of the Pyramid of Quetzalcoatl in Teotihuacán, but Teotihuacán is not just a sacred site in Mexico. It symbolizes the entire world.

You can create a substitute for the Plaza of Quetzalcoatl by making an altar in your own home which will function as the exit from hell. The real meaning of any altar is to suggest a route to God. Every altar can be an exit from hell and a way to God. The altar in the church is also the Eye of God, as is the Pyramid in Teotihuacán. An altar is that place where you feel God's observation of your inmost soul.

The Ceremony

Miguel Ruiz:

To do this ceremony, find a place in nature where you feel connected to the earth, where you can see the sky. You will find the perfect place to carry out your ceremony. This could be on a mountain or beside the ocean or simply in your own yard or a park.

Walk around your Ocean of Hell and pick up seven little pebbles in your left hand. These represent the material things you have collected on your Island of Hell.

Collect seven stones in your right hand. These represent your emotional attachments.

Sit quietly and bring to mind the many things in life that bind you to hell.

When you feel ready, stand up. Say a prayer to your particular angel asking this angel of God to be alive in you.

The only thing keeping you in hell is your attachments. When you feel strong enough to relinquish them, you are ready to continue the ceremony.

Gradually let go of the rocks in your hands as you visualize detaching yourself from those material and emotional bonds that keep you in hell.

For a moment, you will feel a new freedom, but then you will notice that you are still in the material world. Yet there is a new consciousness inside of you. You have an awareness that you have died to the dream of hell. You now know that you are dead.

Imagine yourself walking now across the Ocean of Hell in safety.

Ahead of you are the steps to the Temple of Quetzalcoatl. Feel the connection here to God.

As you leave hell, you enter into the spirit of God, or the Divine, by any name that you give to it.

In effect, with this ceremony, you have died to your former life, but the ceremony can be repeated many times on one's path toward heaven on earth.

II. Crossing the River of Death

Once you have made an initial inventory of your belief system and you have attempted to release your material and emotional attachments, you are ready to exit from hell and proceed through the body of the snake.

Your path is to climb out of the plaza of the Pyramid of Quetzalcoatl to the Avenue of the Dead and turn to the right. You will soon come to the San Juan River, known as the River of Death. The builders of Teotihuacán altered the course of this river so that it would cross the Avenue of the Dead at a right angle.

The assumption is made that you, as a spiritual seeker, have not come to a perfect understanding of your death, but a line has been crossed. As soon as you become aware of your death to the world of illusion, you cannot return to ignorance.

The following ceremony is the second stage in the process of being eaten by the snake.

The Ceremony

Miguel Ruiz:

Imagine yourself going into the underground as a dead person. Only those who are aware that they are dead can cross the river. You are going to cross the River of Death, which compares to the Greek River Styx in Hades, across which Charon ferried the souls of the dead. Your crossing of the river is similar to the three-day passage of Jesus in the tomb, or Odin's hanging in the Tree of Death.

III. The Place of Temptation

The third stage of the journey is the ceremony at the Place of Temptation held on the small temple in the midst of the first plaza to the north of the San Juan River. To reach this plaza, you must climb up the stepped wall that crosses the Avenue and down into the grassy plaza. The temple is a short way ahead. Go there and climb up the stairs to the flat top of the temple. Here it is filled with dirt and a few pebbles and weeds. Whatever structure it might have had on it was probably made of wood and palm fronds. Materially, it did not survive time, but the spirit of the temple remains.

Miguel calls the temple the Island of Temptation. Here, you will take on the role of the spiritual warrior. You will battle against your remaining tenacious attachments.

Before performing the ceremony you will need to quiet your mind and review your progress. The temptation to remain in the dream of hell is a strong one. Although you as a pilgrim have already made efforts to liberate yourself from fear, once again in the Place of Temptation, you will ponder the relationship between the dream, death, and a life of perfect freedom. Is there something holding you back and forcing you to cling to the dream? Consider the question silently.

The Ceremony

Miguel Ruiz:

Surrender to death. Just let go. What is past is dead. We live in the moment. Usually, the Angel of Death will bring us something better than what we have surrendered. The Angel of Death stays behind us throughout our life, eating away the moment we have just traversed and making it possible for us to constantly move into the future. However, we must establish our awareness of the moment between past and future, and center ourselves in it.

We are at a pivotal point in our journey. Until we have been successful in our surrender to death, the snake will not allow us to proceed any further.

Say a prayer to the Mother Earth and offer her your flesh and bones.

Offer the flesh and bones of all your ancestors, as well. By doing so you give them a chance to avoid returning to hell. In this way, the living can give the dead a gift.

Ask Mother Earth to use your flesh and bones as a sacrifice to clean the forest and the rocks.

Dig your own grave in the dirt using a pebble for a shovel. If you cannot go to Teotihuacán, do this ceremony in any soil that is nearby. Mark your grave with a stone. Acknowledge that you, as you previously knew yourself, are actually dead.

This ceremony can be carried out in any quiet place of your choosing. Find a crystal to represent your own body. Dig a small "grave" in the earth and bury your crystal. Cover it well. Say prayers over the crystal as if it were yourself. Include your ancestors in your prayers. Extend your prayers to the earth itself.

When troubles overcome you later, go back to your "grave" and recover the peace of knowing you have died to temptation and are now free to go forward. Your grave will become a source of strength. Remember "I am now dead. I don't have to suffer from those events or people who continue to tempt me."

The Place of the Woman

Before leaving this plaza, there is a discovery to be made. On the left where the women climbed is a temple that does not reveal its importance from the ground level. You must be led around behind the platform to explore the hidden depths of the complex. Miguel calls it the Place of the Woman.

Miguel has seen in visions that women who lived impeccable lives were chosen to live in this enclosure. Across from their area, males also lived a devoted life of purity. Both groups were spiritual warriors.

The stepped temple in the Place of the Woman is below ground level. The sides of these steps were smoothly surfaced and painted a vibrant rose. Walls within the underground structure were also painted rose, which is still visible.

Miguel Ruiz:

In the temple, the women celebrated their menses and ovulation times. Their devotion was to the moon. The moon is a mirror that changes its size every day, reflecting a different quantity of light. The amount of moonlight controls the cycles of life in the earth and also the hormonal cycles of a woman's life. Therefore, women are sensitive to moonlight. Most often among early people, the full moon was the signal for ovulation and the new moon was the time the menstrual period began. After months of living together, women's cycles tend to harmonize. This is still true for women in dormitories and close living conditions.

A woman who surrendered to a shared life in this compound had the intention of becoming the goddess. She gained in self-respect and love. Her purpose was not to procreate. Some of these women, perhaps most of them, came into the spiritual center after their life as mother and wife ended. This was the place for spiritual growth and transcendence.

Two remarkable signs of the spiritual energy in this place remain. Beneath a metal cover that can be lifted up, there is a deep well that looks like a dark vertical tunnel. From the well comes a rush of earthy air. Archaeologists removed a large crystal found at its base. This well is the Vagina, and it is a spiritual birth canal directly into the womb of Mother Earth.

Around the corner from this place is a trough high on the wall that was used as a shower, carrying water from above. Some women visitors have found that they bleed after spending a little time near this shower. The spiritual energy in this chamber is palpable.

There was a long-lasting practice among women to live in this center in reverence to the Mother Earth. They exerted the spiritual discipline necessary to transform themselves on a personal level, but the whole complex is also symbolic of a universal process.

The universe is a process of eternal reproduction. Every planet is a mother who collaborates in reproduction. She decodifies information from the sun which tells her to create life. Information is brought to earth by God's messengers, the angels. Light and the angels are the same.

Mother Earth receives the message in the light that comes from the sun, and she covers "the egg of the soul" with a human body. Inside the egg is the light of the spirit, the angel light sent from the sun. What we really are is the reproduction of angels or the reproduction of sunlight. We are each an angel growing into an egg, which is the soul. At the same time, we have an outer egg filled with spirit that connects with the entire cosmos. We are also a material form of our body.

We could say that DNA, the basic information of life, is condensed light. Earth, the mother, translates DNA into all forms of life. Each form of light has its specific vibration of light. One such vibration from sunlight is for human beings. DNA is an informational packet in sunlight. It is received, modified, and transformed by the earth. The Place of the Woman reflects this elemental process.

The Ceremony

Miguel Ruiz:

In this place, women create a ceremony of acceptance.

A group of women can create this ceremony together or you can create this ceremony privately. You will stimulate your connection to the Place of the Woman if you put a few objects in front of you for contemplation that signify the beauty of the feminine, such as a statuette of a goddess or the Madonna. A photograph of your wedding, pictures of your husband and your children, a lighted candle, perhaps a flower, will turn a nearby table into an altar. The reason for using these sacramentals is to establish a sense of a sacred place.

With your eyes closed, accept the Goddess that exists in you.

> Accept the woman that you are.
> Accept the little girl that you were.
> Accept yourself as the wife.
> Accept yourself as the mother.
> Accept yourself as the Goddess.

Accept yourself just the way you are. You are the being who is half of the reproduction of life. You are the one who carries the fire. You are the one who has the sensitivity to give yourself totally to your groom in your marriage with God in eternal life.

IV. The Place of the Water

You climb over the next stepped wall into a second plaza that has no temples inside it. This is the Place of the Water.

The mind will split here. Emotions that grow from love will be absorbed by your soul. Emotions that grow from fear will return to hell.

In Miguel's dream, the warrior guardian of Paradise cuts the remaining emotions from fear away from the dead spirit and allows it to go forward into the spiral that leads to the Tree of Eternity. This stage of the Avenue of the Dead echoes Miguel's dream. It resembles baptism, when the soul renounces Satan. It symbolizes full trust in God. In the Christian heritage, Jesus became the Christ at baptism. The Place of the Water has a similar result.

Miguel Ruiz:

Your thinking is usually out of control, like a wild horse. At the Place of the Water, you surrender your mind. The mind is not of any use to you now. Information that you need is in your soul. After you go through a ceremony here, you will find you do not need to think in the habitual way any more.

Knowledge is the description of the dream of hell. Knowledge is our last barrier because it describes an illusion. Trying to "know" everything is what holds back our progress toward heaven on earth. Wisdom leads us forward. Once you let go of knowledge, you have nothing left to defend. Everyone's truth becomes valid. This is wisdom.

The digestion of the snake continues to dissolve all of you that is nonessential. You become an angel who requires only the energy of love for your growth.

The Ceremony

Miguel Ruiz:

Visualize that you are beside a great pool of water. Remind yourself that you are approximately seventy percent water. Also remember that all of your emotions are like an Ocean of Hell that is now clear. Imagine Jesus or Buddha as a living ocean of love. They retain their bodies but they are completely free of expectations from others. They are free of fears and filled with love. These avatars represent our own possible future.

Become aware of yourself as a soul covered by an egg. The egg is covered by your mind, which is the sum total of all your emotions. You are gradually leaving your body and you are leaving the fear-based emotions that attach you to your body. Send back any remaining traces of negative emotions to the Ocean of Hell in the Plaza of Quetzalcoatl.

Pray to the Mother Earth and offer the water from your body to her. If it is her will, ask her to use our bodily water to purify all the water we contaminated when we used to live in hell . . . the rain, the snow, the lakes, the rivers, the oceans.

In the distant past, thousands of people went through the ceremony of water at Teotihuacán and for a time at that place, it was truly heaven on earth.

When your ceremony is complete, see yourself as an angel or a beam of light.

V. The Place of the Air

Along the ledges of the third plaza is the Place of the Air. There was once a school here and dwellings. This is also the Place of the Soul. The symbol for this place which signifies the emergence of the soul is an egg from which protrudes the head of a baby eagle. The same symbol is found around the world. Now that you have been altered and you have surrendered your fears, your emotions from hell, your mind, and your body, you are almost purely your soul. You have gone beyond polarity. The process of digestion is completed here.

The Ceremony

Miguel Ruiz:

Breathe deeply and feel the air entering and leaving the body. Recall your first breath. Breathing is a way to communicate with God. With a prayer to the Mother Earth, offer your last breath to cleanse her atmosphere of all pollution.

Remember to be grateful for your breath. As you learn to live in the moment, you will become aware of your breathing and it will be easier to focus on it during your meditation. Before leaving the Place of the Air, stop to meditate upon your breath and to give thanks for it.

VI. The Place of the Fire

You leave the third plaza and enter the fourth one. This is the Place of the Fire. Here is where your spirit is released. You become one within yourself and you find your divinity.

This plaza is comparable to the Chakra of the Heart in the Indian system. It is the energy center of the heart.

The Ceremony

Miguel Ruiz:

Put yourself in the Place of the Fire and go through the ceremony in your mind.

All of the men in the group climb the small temple that faces the plaza on the east.

All of the women climb to the top of the western temple.

Take your time to feel the male and female nature that identifies the physical form you inhabit in this life.

Acknowledge that the opposite of your gender forms a part of your nature, your personality, your inner mind, and subconscious.

Climb down from the temple and meet in the middle of the plaza. Exchange hugs with your opposites. Experience a sense of oneness with others and within yourself.

For this journey to be successful, each participant must reach a feeling of unconditional love for self and other. This ceremony of acceptance helps to build a bridge over the usual separation of the sexes, and it reduces the polarity in interpersonal relationships.

The deeper polarity which separates the divine from the animal in everyone is also bridged. You have crossed that bridge, and now the you that exists is no longer an animal but is a pure spirit. You are growing into yourself as an angel.

To carry out a similar ceremony, you might want to share with a partner of the opposite gender. Each of you can meditate on the polarity of masculine and feminine within each person. Build an inner bridge to join your own masculine and feminine nature. Then share openly with your partner.

VII. The Place of the Recollection

You have arrived at the next plaza where there is no interior temple. This is the Place of the Recollection. All your past lives come into one now. The angel within you grows and creates an etheric double of you.

The etheric double becomes the vehicle for all leftover fears, and the angel becomes one with the universe.

The Ceremony

Miguel Ruiz:

Close your eyes and walk through the grassy plaza with trust as your guide. In these moments, project yourself as far as possible and you will have the sensation of being an enormous spirit, no longer divided but connected with everything in the universe.

Your light body must grow. Expand your sense of your etheric body. Create an etheric double of yourself. Concentrate on this ghostly clone and tell it to expand to the furthest reaches of the universe.

Your etheric double carries the last vestiges of fear that still cling to you as you move through the Avenue of the Dead. You are now free of these fears and are fully prepared to travel onward to the second head of the snake.

VIII. The Pyramid of the Moon

You will pass the Pyramid of the Sun and move directly now to the Pyramid of the Moon. Lawrence Andrews describes it as the Place of Sacrifice. Sense its feminine energy. Try to contact the Smoky Mirror in your own mind. Cynthia Wooton says this energy is ". . . the gentle force of love that unifies with patience, respect and kindness, and that leads us through the labyrinths of our minds to oceans of microcosms that flow into infinity."

In this culmination of your journey along the Avenue of the Dead, you will conduct a sacrificial ceremony.

The Ceremony

Miguel Ruiz:

Imagine that your etheric double is now expanded to the size of the universe itself.

At the base of the Pyramid of the Moon, offer your etheric double to the Mother Earth. Your etheric double is a sacrifice for your own freedom.

Sense its dissolution into the ether that flows through space.

As your etheric double disappears, you are left in a pure, transformed state.

The second head of the snake is here, filling the plaza. Climb the steps of the pyramid to the top. Stop and meditate there, recognizing that your journey is nearly over. You and your angel nature are one.

Climb down, knowing that in doing this you are exiting from the snake.

Feel yourself transformed. It is in this place that one can become the Master of Transformation.

David Dibble's Story

David Dibble has generously written the following story of an ecstatic experience at the Pyramid of the Moon.

David Dibble:

Miguel and I and a group of his students had been exploring Teotihuacán, and we were all brimming with new insights and experiences. At the end of the Avenue of the Dead, in the powerful pyramids of Teotihuacán, sits the Pyramid of the Moon, the pure feminine, the pyramid of love. Before climbing the steps to the top of this beautiful structure, Miguel taught us that it is traditional to meditate and give thanks for the love that we were about to receive from the sculpted rocks that form the pyramid.

During my meditation, I felt an energy that caused me to open my eyes and yet continue to meditate. I watched Miguel slowly climb the stairs to the highest accessible point on the pyramid and sit cross-legged, looking out on all of Teo. As I continued to gaze at Miguel, his body began to disappear into a faint blue haze. The haze became sharply brilliant where Miguel had been seated, the most divine light I had ever seen. Then, something happened that expanded my consciousness to unprecedented levels.

The entire Pyramid of the Moon turned from rock to light, a vibrating blue light so exquisitely beautiful that my only reaction was to sob quietly in profound gratitude for the gift of this communion with spirit. A moment later, I had the experience of merging with the light, internalizing the realization that there was only One. The bliss came in waves as my body disappeared, transformed into the light that is everything. As my body began to reappear, so did Miguel's. Spontaneously, I thrust my hands to the sky in a salute to God that I could express in no other way. I looked up at Miguel and he, too, had his arms stretched to the heavens. We were One.

XI. The Palace of the Butterfly and the Palace of the Jaguars

Anthropologists call the complex to the west of the Pyramid of the Moon the Palace of the Butterfly and the Palace of the Jaguar. To Miguel, they are the heaven of Quetzalcoatl. The Palace of the Butterfly is a big, beautiful building of two stories comprised of many small rooms where male and female masters once lived.

Miguel Ruiz:

During the highly developed spiritual period at Teotihuacán, the masters did not cohabit as sexual partners. They had transcended their physical nature and lived in a sustained spiritual state.

When he enters this area, Miguel feels his connection with these masters. He believes they are alive and their energy can still be perceived there by those who reach the same vibration of love that they felt. Many of his apprentices have been moved by feeling this energy in themselves. The naguals in training who are Dreamers can actually see them and dream with them. The masters welcome them. Tourists do not perceive the vibrations of love in the palace, but when we are into that love, we feel it is like home. We have a connection with the rocks themselves. This is one of the few places where you can see the dream of heaven on earth. That dream had a complete realization for more than a thousand years in Teotihuacán, around two thousand to three thousand years ago.

Miguel Ruiz:

The dream was realized in other places as well. At an earlier date, around five thousand to six thousand years ago in Ancient Egypt, there were masters who maintained the dream of heaven. In Greece around the time of Pythagoras, 600–500 B.C.E., there was a limited school of masters. Most recently, around fifteen thousand years ago, a few lamas in Tibet were illuminated. The flowering of masters in Tibet, Teotihuacán, and Greece all took place during the age of the Fifth Sun.

The Butterfly Ceremony

Miguel Ruiz:

If you are with a group, form a circle in the little plaza that is open directly to the sun. This is the place of the Communion of Love with the Sun.

Communicate with the sun until you feel it is a strong connection with God.

Turn to one another and hug each other in the center of the plaza.

Energy will begin to rise from the base of the spine upwards towards the head. In India, this is known as the kundalini energy. As you leave the Palace of the Butterfly, you may sense the energy of the original Toltec masters.

The Palace of the Jaguars is adjacent to the Palace of the Butterfly. The Palace of the Jaguars holds the same energy as that of all the avatars who have lived on earth. If a follower of the Buddha goes into the palace with awareness, he or she will perceive the Buddha. A Christian will perceive Christ. On occasion, non-Christians perceive Christ, also.

The holiest place in the entire world is the Portal in the Palace of the Jaguars at Teotihuacán. The Portal is enhanced with frescos on either side of the opening which include images of seashells and feathers. At the Portal, you are in the presence of God.

You feel what Moses felt on the mountain when he received the Ten Commandments. We can feel the energy of the Christ clearly in this place.

The Jaguar Ceremony

Miguel Ruiz:

Stand quietly before the Portal. Allow yourself to feel a communication with the divine energy that emanates from this place.

The communication with this energy is always at an emotional level, not in words. The experience of being in the presence of the energy is at its height just in front of the Portal or just inside it.

Nothing more is needed.

X. The Pyramid of the Sun

Lawrence Andrews has written, "The final process in the Path of Freedom, the Mastery of Intent, was undertaken at the Pyramid of the Sun, a place dedicated to transcending the limits of the human experience. Here one merged one's own intent (or nagual as it was also called) with the intent of being of the Sun." (*Magical Blend*, ibid.)

Miguel Ruiz:

We save the Pyramid of the Sun for a direct communication from the earth to the sun. The intent of the Pyramid of the Sun is to help you find your personal vibration of light in the whole river of light that the masters can see flowing between the sun and the earth. Here you will have communion with your personal ray of light.

The Toltec masters went to the top of the Pyramid of the Sun and merged with their personal ray of light and virtually disintegrated their bodies as they ascended into the sun.

From the air, the Pyramid of the Sun can be seen as the upside down figure of a man, similar to Jesus on the cross. His head appears to be the platform at the bottom of the pyramid. His arms are outstretched along the two staircases of the bottom tier. His torso is the center of the pyramid, and his legs are the top staircase.

The Ceremony

Miguel Ruiz:

Before climbing, the group goes onto the platform that sits in front of the pyramid. Here they say goodbye to earth.

The nagual presses the closed eyes of each person in the group so each one will be able to see as a nagual. He or she asks them to find a personal rhythm of breathing and to begin practicing it.

The women start walking to the right and go around the pyramid. The men walk around it on the left. Usually, the right side is male and the female is left, but here we deliberately use the opposite side of our own gender.

This passage awakens the pyramid.

As you walk, look about three feet ahead.

You will perceive three levels of energy at differing speeds. One level is on the exterior of the pyramid. Another is along the path you are walking.

The third is in the pyramid itself. Your will is connected with the pyramid.

By the time you reach the top, your perception will have changed.

At the top of the pyramid, according to instructions given to each person, one couple sits in the center back to back with knees raised. One couple faces inward from each side.

The rest of the group form circles around these figures.

Find your inner silence.

From the silence, we start to create the vibrations of sound.

Begin to hum. A large sound will develop. It will not be organized. The effort is to become one and to merge with the pyramid. Anything can happen during this final ceremony.

Although the journey along the Way of Death at Teotihuacán is designed to release a person from fear, there is always a reoccurence of what Miguel calls the Parasite that still connects you with hell. He has become a master, yet he continues to make the journey to Teotihuacán to cleanse the smallest bit of his mind that might still hold the poison of wounds from the dream of hell. He has innovated a new practice for himself that involves taking the whole journey backwards, beginning at the Pyramid of the Sun and finally returning to the Palace of Quetzalcoatl. It is his way of challenging himself with an increasingly severe inventory.

Miguel Ruiz:

Even though the Parasite is no longer in control, the Toltec warrior recognizes that there is a Parasite attempting to sabotage spiritual progress. It is possible to convert a Parasite into an Ally. If this happens, the Ally facilitates spiritual growth and the warrior feels like he or she is making a new beginning.

With the help of the Ally, the warrior will be able to clean each and every wound with complete honesty. It is not possible to undergo this level of truth until reaching mastery. It is a painful process.

CHAPTER ELEVEN

THE WAYS OF THE NAGUAL
IN THE WORLD

MASTERY OF THE SILENT knowledge opens one's channel to the energy of the nagual, which is a living spirit that inhabits an infinite expanse throughout the universe. Nagual energy increases awareness and intent to such a degree that a master of silent knowledge can break free from the dream of hell that controls the world to become filled with loving energy.

While learning the masteries of Toltec wisdom, the spiritual warrior may feel he or she is on a solitary path of self-improvement through self-discipline. It would seem that the only beneficiary of such dedication is the individual master. However, this is not the case. Once a person has come to a state of freedom from the first attention into a state of love, that person can then serve in the world by being an agent of transformation. The master can teach others to follow a similar path by simply being a person in a state of love.

An agent has obligations to fulfill a mission. A nagual's mission is to practice all the masteries acquired during apprenticeship and share wisdom with others. Like yeast in bread dough, nagual masters will help in the great transition that is taking place on earth today from a dense level of chaos into a new level of peace and creativity.

After graduating from medical school, Miguel had to serve at a public clinic in the desert. While there, he studied nagualism with a discarnate teacher sent to him by his grandfather. This old wiseman made Miguel face his fears in numerous frightening encounters. Based on those experiences, Miguel used to teach differently from the way he does now. In his earliest classes he exposed his students to dangerous or fearful situations. Then Sarita showed Miguel what it means to practice unconditional love and he saw that love works far better than fear to develop spiritual mastery.

The inventory is the basic discipline in Miguel's approach to changing the dream to a dream of heaven on earth. The inventory is a solution to recognizing our fears without confronting fearful situations. The inventory is a private pursuit. It can take as long as one needs, and it can be repeated many times. It can even take place in our dreams. Dreaming is our human task. It goes on night and day. One of the benefits of Toltec training is that we can learn to change our dream.

Miguel instructs his apprentices to prepare to dream in this way:

1. When you fall asleep, keep your awareness so that you can control your dream.
2. Practice power dreaming in which you change the dream you are having. You will become aware that you are the dream and the dreamer.
3. Notice that your dreaming body is different from your ordinary body.
4. Begin to create a dream of heaven. Demons will try to stop you, but remember you are experiencing the dream you are creating, so create the most beautiful possible dream.
5. When you reach a state of bliss, you become the God of pure love. With love, you will have your reunion with God.

Miguel's students become his fellow teachers. Cynthia Wootton is now a nagual who practices the Toltec Masteries. She lists four masteries instead of the usual three. Her fourth is Mastery of Dreaming.

Wootton writes, "Miguel's purpose is to help as many human beings achieve their full enlightened potential (as possible) so that they can manifest their power to create an inner and outer world of harmony and balance in the lifestyle of their choice."

Wootton says that her studies with Miguel have transformed her life. "I have joined with Miguel and a few others in dedicating my life to making these teachings known. There is no doubt in my mind that human beings must evolve. When we achieve our infinite nature, we feel a fulfillment which allows us to have a vision of heaven on earth. Miguel, myself, and some others have chosen to join forces to create this new dream of heaven for ourselves and anyone else who is ready."

In her written statement, Wootton gives a fresh understanding of the masteries. Writing about the Mastery of Awareness, she says, "As we evolve, the etheric energy we create reflects subtler and more varied qualities of spiritual energy. What do we mean by spiritual energy? It is that undifferentiated energy in which we perceive oneness with everything around us. The feeling we have from the experience of spirit is divine love, ecstasy, or infinite freedom. This mastery brings us face to face with choices to break free from all that limits us."

Of the Mastery of Stalking, Wootton explains that it is the basis of the spiritual warrior's way of life. "We begin to watch our thoughts, words, or actions to see why and how we limit ourselves, we suffer and feel unhappiness."

With the Mastery of Dreaming, Wootton explains that we gain control over the energy that goes into dreaming this "fixed reality" day in and day out. Once we start using the etheric energy at our disposal, ". . . there are no limits to the explorations we can make into other realities by means of what can be called etheric or astral traveling. When we perceive etheric energy, we perceive a greater portion of the totality of being than when we perceive (only) physical energy."

The Mastery of Intent, Wootton says, is "the final mastery. . . . It is the mastery of the totality of being."

This book is a tool to spread the possibility of creating a new dream farther and wider. Around the world there are other traditions and teachers doing the same work as Miguel. When a sufficient number of people accept the change in world view that allows them to live free of guilt, judgment, worry, and unhappiness, the entire earth will be more in balance. The changed vibrations then emitted by earth will affect the solar vibration in sunlight and, in turn, affect the rest of the universe.

Change begins within a single mind. You might be the one person needed to encourage and hasten the turning toward peace on the planet.

Miguel advises his apprentices to begin taking students of their own to teach them the art of stalking and to lead them on trips to Teotihuacán. In this way, Miguel magnifies the effect of his own teaching.

Certain key teachings are making their way further and further into the psyche of all shamanic students. It is for this moment in history that shamanism has survived, so that teachers like Miguel can assist with the change of global consciousness that is in progress.

One of Miguel's most important contributions as a nagual is the link he has made between Toltec wisdom and other spiritual traditions, particularly Buddhism and Christianity.

Miguel's Story of the Buddha

Miguel Ruiz:

The story of Buddha is similar to the story of Jesus. Buddha was born and named Siddhartha. He was a prince and he was to be a king to conquer all of India. When he was born, the astrologers predicted he would be either the greatest king or an ascetic who travels to hell and brings back the secrets of hell to teach the world.

His father tried to protect Siddhartha. He created a beautiful world for him. He arranged for him to marry at a young age and to have a child. He wanted to force him to remain human. But the father could not prevent Siddhartha from reaching his destiny. He was strong, young, and powerful. He left his secluded palace and went out into the village where he saw suffering. He asked, "Why did you lie to me?" His father said, "I don't want you to suffer."

Siddhartha felt compassion and he felt guilt. "I have to see what they feel," he said. He wanted to see what it really meant to be human. This led him to hell. He had judgments against his father and others and he felt the need to be punished. He went into the life of an ascetic and he begged for charity. He was so compassionate that all the beggars joined him. He brought them hope. Then he discovered that he was guiding them in the wrong way. He began eating again and he recovered his strength. The others felt betrayed by him.

So he went alone into the jungle and he found one of the wisest trees that ever lived. It was one thousand years old. He studied the tree and saw the mind of the tree. He saw that light is really the knowledge. He experienced ecstasy. Then he became the Buddha. He went into trance and absorbed knowledge from the tree.

Trees' minds are close to humans' minds. The tree became the guide of Buddha. Buddha saw that this is all a dream and it is alive. In the dream were gods who ruled the dream. He saw the total evolution of all humans. He saw that it is almost hopeless to try to escape from the dream. For the gods, creation, and development, it is even more hopeless than it is for humans to change the dream. The gods control the humans and lead them to the nightmare. All the gods of fear created evil.

Buddha saw that getting out of the dream is to become light and to become God.

He said that our destiny is to transcend.

Buddha had a moment of choice. He could: 1. Be light, be God, ascend. 2. Go back and share the vision. His compassion was so great he decided to go back. Then the dream attacked him, just as Jesus was tempted with sexuality. Buddha saw everyone shoot at him with bows and arrows. The arrows symbolized their criticism and gossip about him. The arrows turned into flowers. This happened five hundred years before Christ.

In the State of Oaxaca in Mexico, there is a famous huge tree called Tule. That is the wisest tree I have ever seen. It has the energy of the father. You can feel the love from it. There are few birds in it and they are usually silent.

Beside the Tule is another, smaller tree, which is female. It has the energy of the mother. It is filled with birds.

Gaya says that when people circle the Tule tree they come to a point of facing the tree. It lifts them up and pulls them off their feet.

The Tule is the guru or wise teacher among trees. It is the keeper of the silent knowledge.

Miguel's Vision of Christ

While he was an apprentice with Sarita, Miguel stayed in trance for hours at a time. Among his visions were his encounters with the story of Jesus' life that he saw as if he were a witness. For this to happen, he had to align with Jesus' energy vibration and then he could live the story emotionally.

Miguel Ruiz:

The Jesus I found in my meditations was ninety percent different from the Jesus presented in his church. I do not agree with the last fifteen hundred years of Christianity at all.

The original Christianity was when Jesus was in his body. He taught a way of life almost exactly like the Toltecs. Jesus gave us immense gifts.

He gave us forgiveness. Forgiveness was his way of cleaning the poison from our mind, like the inventory. Forgiveness is the only way to heal the roots of all the emotional poison that we have.

Forgiveness is an act of self-love. Once you forgive, there will be scars there, but you will not hurt. Forgiveness is the great gift from Jesus.

The whole culture in Jesus' time was placing blame. The Jewish religion was still barbarian. In the temple, they had to sacrifice animals to a bloody god. In the Bible, Moses describes how to make a sacrifice, how to dispense the blood in the tabernacle, how to burn the sacrifice. It was fanatical. They followed the letter, not the spirit, of the law. They believed in a judging god.

Jesus was in conflict with this religion that preached fear of a God who is jealous and will punish you.

Jesus practiced love. This is his main gift. He did not say "an eye for an eye," he said to "love your neighbor as yourself."

It was not easy for Jesus to teach his knowledge to those who did not want to hear it, so he taught in parables. He made his listeners understand with love. While he talked, they were trancelike and they shared the silent knowledge of unconditional love.

Jesus was really a king from the dynasty of David. The Romans had put a false king in place. Those in the House of David expected a messiah to recover the kingdom.

Jesus' real father was a Zealot, a rebel warrior named Judas. He tried to overthrow the Romans but he failed and was killed. He did not know that Mary was pregnant when he died. Mary was just a teenaged girl. Those who were in the House of David expected her to bear a son who would continue the lineage. They chose a husband for her who would be a father to her child. Joseph was a priest of the temple who was a teacher. He was in his eighties. Mary married Joseph, and Jesus gained the spiritual instruction he needed when Joseph took Jesus to Egypt at a young age. The community did not expect Jesus to reject being a king.

Jesus joined the Essenes, but he already had the silent knowledge and he was more liberal than the Essenes.

The Essenes were waiting for the end of the world at any moment. They tried to be clean and pure to be ready when the Master of Justice arrived.

Jesus said, "I am the Master of Justice and this is not the end of the world." The Essenes kicked Jesus and John the Baptist out of their community.

Two forces worked on Jesus. One told him to become the king. The other told him to change the beliefs of his community.

The Jewish people were worshiping a force in the temple that was not God. Jesus was dangerous to the Pharisees who saw that he was very well-known as the probable messiah, but they denied it.

Jesus began going in a different direction from what his followers expected. He did not choose to be king, but to profess love, forgiveness, and truth. Then his image changed and many saw him as a prophet.

He began thinking of himself as a son of God, although not the only son. In Israel the ideal was monotheistic, but in other countries at the time, such as Rome, Egypt, and Greece, there was a belief in semi-gods. Caesar proclaimed himself God. Therefore, it was not weird for Jesus to say he was a son of God. He said we are God's children. He said God is love and forgiveness rather than a god to fear. They had thought of God as remote. Jesus said, "I am the son of man. You are my brothers. God is our father. My father doesn't want sacrifices."

The people loved and followed him. The ideas he taught were a threat to the temple and the temple leaders wanted him gone, although many priests favored Jesus. They knew that with Jesus they could be free. There were many meetings in the temple.

Jesus spoke of bringing heaven to earth. "My kingdom is not of this world. It is a place of love where everyone is kind," he said.

His apostles were excited about arriving in Jerusalem. They thought they would be victors and Jesus would proclaim himself the king. The temple expected him to say this. If he did, there was no way the Pharisees could stop him. They invited Jesus to the Sanhedrin, which was the highest judicial and ecclesiastical council of the nation with seventy members. He said, "No, I will not become the king. Do not tempt me." He predicted the crowd would kill him. This was to be his destiny.

The Resurrection was another gift from Jesus. It means the awakening from the dream. The Resurrection is the opposite of Adam and Eve's eating from the fruit of the Tree of Life.

An ancient tradition that began in Egypt is the Communion. Originally, the communion wafer represented Ra, the Sun God, or Horus, who was the same as Jesus. Wine represented the Holy Blood, or the specific ray of light that created all humans. Wine and bread were used in the Egyptian ritual in the same way they are in Christian services.

Jesus began a new covenant between man and God. Despite all the corruption of his teaching, the covenant is still valid. The present time of the Sixth Sun is the time of Jesus' prophecy. All events around the world are inseparable. All humans are one organ. What happened in Jerusalem happened in Teotihuacán. Jesus was also Quetzalcoatl.

All avatars speak of love and forgiveness, but Jesus proved these things in action.

For me, the fact that he proved it is of the greatest importance. Jesus taught us how to die as a warrior, even though he was humiliated and hurt, he did not hate. He showed no revenge. He still felt love for everyone. This is the part of Jesus' story that made me feel Jesus is the greatest human who ever lived. The best teaching of Jesus is his unfailing love.

After Jesus died, his followers went in two directions. One group saw Jesus as the messiah, like a king, and they wanted to preserve his lineage. Jesus' wife and son were taken to the south of France and then to England. The story of the Holy Grail is the continuation of the House of David. Holy Grail means Holy Blood. The Crusades were started to reestablish the kingdom for the messiah. The secret societies of Masonry and the Rosicrucians, Knights Templar, and Le Catars, as well as King Arthur's Round Table were all connected to the House of David.

The other group, the Apostles, saw Jesus as the son of God and they kept his teachings. They were persecuted, but they founded seven churches. The big victory of Christianity was when one of the Roman caesars around 200 A.D. declared that he was the pope and head of the Christian church. He mixed the ideas of Jesus with those of another movement in Rome at that time called the Victorious Sun. In this group, they worshiped a man who comes from the sun and wins over evil. He also was a son of God. After that, everybody had to be Christian and to support the religion. They sent emissaries to find out about Jesus. The caesar only accepted four of the versions of Jesus' life, and those were considered the evangelists'. The other reports were the Apocrypha, never accepted officially. All the old gods were renamed saints.

These facts will be legitimized soon by scholarship. There has always been discord between the Catholic church and the secret groups, such as the Templars, but soon all the information will come out and the image of Jesus will change. The Great Imperium will break when the papacy comes to an end. They will discover ruins in the south of France and they will see that there were messages hidden in the art of Michelangelo and Leonardo, as well as many other artists. The revelation has already begun. The seals, mentioned in the Book of Revelations, will be broken. Some are already broken. The first seal is hell.

The Bible and the Toltecs' Silent Knowledge

In the first chapters of the Gospel according to John, Miguel sees "pure esoteric knowledge from the mystery school of the Christians." Verse by verse, the statements are kindred in language and meaning to the Toltecs' silent knowledge.

As Miguel has said, there is just one silent knowledge and it is being revealed all over the world. This is not the first time the silent knowledge has been revealed. What is new is that our contemporary interpretation of the ancient wisdom is influenced by scholarship and scientific knowledge from recent times. The following Biblical quotation is from the Authorized King James version.

Miguel Ruiz:

1. In the beginning was the Word, and the Word was with God, and the Word was God. 2. The same was in the beginning with God. 3. All things were made by him; and without him was not any thing made that was made. 4. In him was life; and the life was the light of men. 5. And the light shineth in darkness; and the darkness comprehended it not. . . .

9. *That* was the true Light, which lighteth every man that cometh into the world. 10. He was in the world, and the world was made by him, and the world knew him not. 11. He came unto his own, and his own received him not. 12. But as many as received him, to them gave he power to become the sons of God, *even* to them that believe on his name: 13. which were born, not of blood, nor of the will of the flesh, nor of the will of man, but of God. 14. And the Word was made flesh, and dwelt among us (and we beheld his glory, the glory as of the only begotten of the Father,) full of grace and truth. . . .

Everything comes from the word and this is exactly the same as intent and the will. Everything comes from light. Light is energy. In the Toltec, we say that intent is that quality of the energy that allows all energy to transform. Everything is an emanation of the one spirit.

"Which were born, not of blood, nor of the will of the flesh, nor of the will of man, but of God." This means of the will, or the intent, of God.

"In him was life; and the life was the light of men." Life and light are exactly the same, which is the basic knowledge that the Toltecs taught. We are only life. Without the life that is in us, our bodies would decay.

The light shines in the dark. Darkness is matter. Light works through matter but matter resists. It does not "comprehend" the light. Matter resists the light and this resistance makes matter grow.

The Bible says, "He was not in the world, but he came into the world and the world did not know him." Our own body does not accept our light, our energy. When the Bible says that "He came into his own and his own received him not," that compares with the Toltec truth that the light of divinity comes to us and we resist it and we stay in the world of illusion. "Whoever receives the light becomes the children of God," compares exactly with the meaning of Teotihuacán, the place where we become God, but this can only happen when we surrender to the light.

Miguel interprets other aspects of the Bible, particularly the warnings of Armageddon in The Revelation of Saint John the Divine, to elements of Toltec lore. Armageddon is signaling the death of the dream of the planet. Destruction by nature or by man-made causes is not inevitable. It can be diverted by the awakening of humans. Miguel believes this awakening is moving very rapidly.

"Where chaos is the worst, awakening is moving faster," Miguel says. "What happens in the world is exactly the same as what happens when a mind awakens. Before there is a sense of peace, there is an increase of chaos."

Miguel Ruiz:

Perhaps one human has a belief system which includes the idea that suffering is normal and all around other humans are suffering, but at a certain moment this person awakens and knows we don't have to suffer. This person faces rejection by changing his belief system. If we are different we aren't accepted. To be different is an act of rebellion. There will be a reaction inside and outside when we move into the unknown. Fears come out and try to stop our transformation. Chaos is the result. Reason is weakened and loses direction. After the crisis passes in the person and in the outside world also, then the individual is able to be himself.

First there is the war in our minds. Here, the Victim sabotages our efforts to change. Our beliefs are our laws.

I had an apprentice who worked with me for many years. She had been widowed many years before. Her beliefs gave her a lot of resistance but she came to a moment of change. Then she went back where she used to live and had her husband's remains exhumed and cremated. When she scattered his ashes she felt free and happy, but her family were surprised and angry. They blamed her and went to their priest. He thought she had done an evil act. For a while, she saw herself through their eyes again, but she let it go and left, taking her happiness and freedom with her.

Until people find God inside, they need to believe in the God who is outside. We are all black magicians, spreading our emotional poison until we learn to be white magicians. Then we convert from fear to love.

Once a person has transformed, he or she does not take things personally. Jesus and Buddha came into the world and they had to make the change to enlightenment. In doing so, they opened higher opportunities for everyone. They were born with all their opportunities, but they had to go into hell just like everyone else. They were fully human.

They lived normal lives in normal circumstances for their times, with a body, mind and soul, but they became light.

We act from fear at first, but once we become aware of what we are doing, the opportunity opens for us to transform. Even in the most direful circumstances such as the concentration camps of World War II, it was possible for people to change from their desire to change.

For the past twenty centuries, Christians have taught that we are our brother's keeper. Miguel gives this worthy ideal a different sort of interpretation from the usual one that is vested in guilt. To be responsible, he says, is to respect each other's way of being. We help each other most by our offer of love. Wherever love is received it will be effective. All we really can do for another is to love him or her. We are not responsible for the actions of another.

Feeling sorry and guilty for others is not effective. When the government gives handouts to people so that they make more money from not working than they can from holding a job, they are destroyed. They are not helped. When people do not work, there is no action. There has to be action in order to have transformation. Without action, the people become bored and boredom leads to crime. We are here to produce.

The Toltec View of Love

Jesus taught that love is the essence of the silent knowledge. The Toltecs also knew that the closer we get to love, the closer we get to God. Love is the opposite of fear. Love is that fire that does not burn, that purifies everything it touches, whereas fear is the fire that burns and destroys everything it touches. It is so difficult to put the meaning of love into words. It is easier to speak of the characteristics of love. In this way, we will see that the characteristics of love and those of fear are exact opposites. We can imagine two tracks, one of love and one of fear. By comparing them, we can see which track we are on. Miguel teaches that pure love is composed of seven characteristics:

1. Love has no expectations.
   Fear is filled with expectations.
2. Love has no obligations.
   Fear is full of obligations. When we act from obligation, our resistance makes us suffer. When we fail to act on our obligations, we feel guilty.
3. Love has respect, not only for others, but also for ourself.

Fear respects nothing, including itself. When I feel sorry for myself, I do not respect myself. When I feel sorry for you, I do not respect you.
4. Love is patient.
Fear is impatient.
5. Love does not pity.
Fear is filled with pity, especially with self-pity.
6. Love is detached.
Fear is filled with attachments and the dread of having to let go.
7. Love is kind.
Fear is too self-involved to be kind.

Relationships based on love are not broken by efforts to control the other. Unconditional love places no burdens on one's partner. From this position, Miguel discusses the need to reconceive the institution of marriage. Chief among changes, he thinks, will be the new relationships that replace the worn out institution of marriage, as we have known it. This system is broken. The new relationship, based on respect, is just beginning. There is complete confusion, worldwide, in human relationships because we are resisting this change, but it will inevitably take place.

Miguel's Special Message

Many voices are calling us to awaken. Couched within their messages are similar warnings. We hear that we are living in an illusion. We learn that the earth is a living being and we must protect her from further degradation. Among the voices are those who tell their listeners who it is we should blame for the misery we see around us. Our parents, white men, the government, the United States, corporations—there is always a guilty party.

Carried to its extreme, the wake-up call gives an impression that each of us is the victim of a corrupt system. If our early victimization can be ascribed to a family member or caretaking adult, we are expected to seek out this memory and bring the pain to the surface of our consciousness . . . and then, what? Miguel brings a different message. Wake up, he tells us, to your personal responsibility. What happens to you is dependent upon your own thoughts. Your actions and reactions are under your control. You are not the Victim nor are you a Judge to lay blame on others. You are a spiritual being empowered with the potential to transform the dream of the planet.

The Toltec system to which Miguel has added the revealed wisdom he receives in trance states is completely devoted to the refinement of the individual. A principle of esoteric wisdom is that no one has power over anyone else's soul and spirit. The awakened individual is one who takes upon him/herself the total responsibility for thought, word, and action.

Awakening in the Toltec way causes deep changes in a person's perception of the world. Fear, guilt, blame, and shame are surpassed. From such a vantage point, the world appears just. Divine order operates at all levels.

The transformed master of Toltec wisdom is not a blissed-out lotus eater whose focus is limited to personal contemplation. If fully realized, mastery is accompanied by practical changes. Talents, drives, and abilities rise in consciousness, fueled by the passion of joy in action.

All of us are talented at birth, but we often squelch the nudges and desires we feel in order to earn a living. In case after case, the Toltec masters find they can earn a living by commitment to their talents. It is a matter of priorities. At the top of the list is expansion of those things that give joy and hence lend positive energy to the person and through the person to the world. Miguel conveys a practical form of spirituality. First, one takes full charge of oneself, cleanses emotional poison from the mind, finds the source of joy, and practices living in heaven on earth.

The practice is akin to an art form. Miguel says all Toltecs were artists; he even says they were supreme artists. We can take that to mean you are living as an artist when your life is a work of art, a conscious, living creation, always in process.

The mark of a Toltec master is self-possession, someone who has risen above the personal and ego-driven, a self-monitoring person who is aware of the power in his or her word, action, and thought. Restraint, which rests on awareness, does not restrict spontaneity. In fact, freedom from fear releases a person's spontaneous response to life. The Toltecs' goal is happiness.

CHAPTER TWELVE

GAYA'S STORY — THE WISDOM OF A NAGUAL WOMAN

Entering the Realm of Magic

I had a dream, a remembrance of a dream, where I was hanging onto something with the edge of my fingers, looking back to my right into a body of water. There was a presence with me who said, "Go on and take your message, but you must be patient. Your message won't be for everyone, but there are those awaiting you." I remember that dream as being a birth dream for me.

I'm not that good at dates, times, and ages, and things like that. I'm very experiential. I just remember as a child that I knew that my message was to tell people that they were God. I never felt free to tell people that until maybe five years ago. It was something I had within myself that I knew was my message.

Around 1987, I was traveling on an airplane when it flew into a thunderstorm. In that moment I realized that I might die. I thought, "I can't die before I awaken. I don't want to die again unless I am fully awakened." I determined for myself in that instant that I was going to go for my liberation. Even if I had to jump out of that airplane — and at the time that was the most frightening thing I could think of — I was willing to do it to awaken because I wanted so badly to be free.

That incident sparked an idea inside me that I needed to work with a shaman. I didn't even know what a shaman was. In a bookstore, I found the magazine *Shaman's Drum* and I read advertisements of trips to Peru and Brazil for working with shamans. Although I was terrified, I signed up for one of those journeys. My husband drove me to the airport. Later he told me that as we sat there waiting for the departure time, he had looked at me and he knew that I would never come home. I never did, although I came home physically.

Now, I know what happened. Everything is in divine order. I did not have a clue what was going on, but I just knew I needed to find my freedom. So, I went to Peru and I worked with Eduardo Calderon for two weeks. He is a wonderful man. The first time I saw him he said, "You will have to become the master of electricity."

I had started to have imbalances in my heart at the beginning of my spiritual awakening. My heart was beating erratically. During surgery, a few years after that, doctors discovered I had mutated an electrical river across the top of my heart. Otherwise, my heart is in perfect shape. In terms of electricity, it is as if my heart is a mutant, so I now have a pacemaker. Calderon could not have known that, but he could see on other levels.

Calderon saw me wrapped in a violet light. The natural color of my auric field is blue, but I have another ring of light around me that is violet — which is Miguel. In every ceremony that we did in Peru, Calderon would come over and honor me in some way. This was because, I found out later, I carry the imprint of the nagual woman. He recognized my energetic imprinting. He also knew that the violet light that wrapped me was a nagual. Calderon asked me about my husband and he realized that the nagual was not my husband. He could see Miguel's mark on me, which is the color violet.

This was my first experience of walking into the world of magic. When I look back on my life, I see that for the past decade I have been living in the realm of magic beyond what my reason can understand and know. After I worked with Calderon we made an agreement that I would come home for three months and then I would return for more study because, with him, I had my first experience of seeing energy directly. He became my teacher by moving my assembly point.

When I came home my heart was bothering me and I went to Miguel's mother Sarita to see if she could help me. She told me later that when she saw me she remembered that five years before she had seen me in her vision, knowing that I would be with Miguel. She had seen me with red hair. At that time, I was dying my hair red. She wanted to know if I were married and I nodded. She asked me, "Do you have children?" and I said, "Yes."

"Well, you have to meet my son Miguel because I am aware that you will want to work with him," she said.

I went outside and asked the woman sitting at the desk if these people were shamans. And she said, "Oh yes, they are Toltec shamans." That didn't make any sense to me, but I asked if Miguel took apprentices. She said, "Yes, but he doesn't take just anybody." Miguel was teaching in this little temple in San Diego when I met him. Miguel told me later that from the age of thirteen, each time he went into states of meditation or felt emotionally distressed, I would come to him. He had expected that when he grew up I would be his wife, but that didn't happen. He kept seeing me in stressful times and he called me his Angel of Death. As soon as he saw me walk into the temple, he was scared and wanted to run.

I did not know what was coming until I sat down and talked with him. Miguel spoke and understood English but not as well as he does now. He worked with Silent Knowledge one-to-one with a client mostly through his hands. When he did body work, he just passed the knowledge and vibration through himself. As soon as he touched my back, I started to have memories of Miguel with me in different situations. In that dream state, I had a vision of a beautiful woman in the form of a green snake with two heads. She was jewel-encrusted. All of a sudden, one of her heads ate the other.

After Miguel was finished, he asked me what my experience had been. I told him my dream and he laughed and said he had been having that dream since he was thirteen or fourteen. We entered into a dynamic. Whenever I was with Miguel or thought about him, I couldn't help scratching my body. I realize now it was my spirit awakening, although I didn't understand it at the time. When I told Miguel, "It feels like you're under my skin," he said, "Yes, I am."

Now I see that everything was coming to the time when we would start the dance that we call the nagual and the nagual woman. We share an energetic and a common vision. His dream is to bring heaven on earth and mine is to help people know their divinity. It was like a perfect marriage. Miguel has consciously recollected us having thirteen lifetimes together. He says that we go back thousands of years and that we are like twin souls. I started to work with him in June. In November, I left my twenty-five-year marriage.

Before I had gone to Peru or met Miguel, while I was riding my stationary bicycle doing my exercises, I felt a presence come to me in the form of a golden light in my mind. In my experience, it was the Christ. I just surrendered myself to it. I said, "I offer myself to be a channel of your light. Please use me in this world."

Three weeks later, I knew of some available land in Fairbanks Ranch, an exclusive area in San Diego where I had already built and sold a home. I was interested in doing that again and I was out with a realtor looking at a four-acre property with a natural ravine in the middle of it when I saw that I could create a lake there. I said, "Take me to the office right now because I'm going to buy this property and make a million dollars." That experience seemed directly connected to the presence on the bike. It was a gift from spirit.

In essence, this inspiration allowed me to claim my freedom. I created a home like a castle. I worked out all the details and hired a builder, but I never saw the finished house. Within two months of breaking ground, it sold just from the diagram. I walked away because my life was all about spirit, about Miguel and about my growth.

Once I started to work with Miguel, I always felt my connection to him above my head. It wasn't the body. My connection with him was so intense I knew I had to be with him, although we had not really talked about that. Eventually, I made a spiritual marriage with Miguel attended by all of our relatives.

On our two-month honeymoon in Mexico, we went to Teotihuacán. This was the beginning of a huge body of work. What happened was that Miguel went very deep into a process. He became completely silent. We were walking along the Avenue of the Dead and I sensed the presence of millions of souls all around us. I was so aware of all these energies moving with us. When I looked down, I saw that half my body was not me. I was in another body wearing sandals. We were silently walking. At the Pyramid of the Moon we climbed to the top. Miguel sat there seeing the two-headed snake. He recollected the energy that we carry as my being Quetzalcoatl and his being Smoky Mirror. I told him about seeing many souls there and that we were literally carrying them with us. He said, "Yes, we are doing that. We are going to go home and start bringing groups of people down here."

He had been so silent, so deep within himself, like a zombie the whole three days we had been there that I teased him, "Miguel, who would want to be with you? I haven't wanted to be with you. You've been a nightmare to be with. You've been so moody and withdrawn." But I believed that we would bring people down there.

Redemption of the Parasite

I want to talk about the Parasite as an aspect of our consciousness which has forgotten its divinity. It is the aspect of our consciousness that has the ability to feel. You could call it the emotional body. It carries all the experiences we have had. Every experience is an individual emotion. Either we pass through it or it is stuck there with us. When we remember our childhood, most of us cannot recollect the wonderful parts of being a child. We remember the negative aspects of our childhood that we have not fully experienced because we blocked them with our defense system. That block is just like glue. We have a judgment that holds an experience like a freeze-frame photograph in our auric field. It is imprinted in our emotional body. The emotion is trapped by judgment. Enlightenment is the state that comes when we reexperience our past completely, without judgment, and everything goes back into light where everything is love, the expression of God.

Here is my experience:

I went to Mexico to visit San Miguel de Allende with my sister so that we could study Spanish. While we were still in Mexico City, I took her to visit the Basilica of the Virgin of Guadalupe, which she had never seen. We walked up the long flight of stairs and then we went inside. As I knelt and looked up at the statue of the Mother, this vision came from her. I saw the Mother with two chalices. One chalice faced the earth and the other chalice faced upward at her heart. I was seeing the birth of the Mother down into the earth. I sensed from the chalice facing upward through her heart that we would be reborn. We would transcend into our Divine Self by the Divine Mother birthing us back into heaven. What I knew at that moment was that in order to make the birth from earth back into heaven, I would have to lead a life like that of the Divine Mother. I would have to have the unconditional love that mothers have for their children. I would have to love every man, woman, and every thing with that same quality of love. The purity of that love doesn't hold any competitiveness, jealousy, fear, or anything negative. I asked myself, how will I ever get there?

We left the Basilica and took a bus to San Miguel. Later, Miguel met me there and we planned to join a group of people who were going to Teotihuacán with us for a power journey. A couple of weeks before we were to leave for Teo, we had a conversation based on something that had happened between us earlier. Because I knew inside myself that this dream I was living with Miguel was dead, I told Miguel he had to let me go. We needed to move into another dream. He did not want to do it, but because I asked him, he said he would. He would cut his emotional ties with me. That was the deepest talk we had ever had.

I felt that in my years with him, I had never given myself one hundred percent to life. Maybe I never had. What I have learned is that the spiritual experiences we think will be glorious and tran-scendent perhaps are not. They can be the worst things you ever will walk through emotionally. Both of us, Miguel and I, had been going through growth experiences since we had been together. At one point, I felt I was there with Miguel's empty body while he was experienc-ing a transformation. It was so bleak for me that afterwards I tried to escape emotionally. I carried an emotional wound from that time, which felt like a betrayal. (My efforts to escape had given Miguel the same feeling of betrayal.)

In this place of truth in our conversation, speaking from the wound, I realized that in our eight years together, my Parasite had been living my life, not the real me. I said, "You know, Miguel, I'm going to ask you to walk with me in relationship where I can use you to be one hundred percent with myself. Every time I come to a place where I want to escape or want to defend, I will stand there. Give me an opportunity to do it." He said he would.

When we were on the bus to Teo, Miguel did not tell me what he was doing, but he performed an act of power. He removed all my defenses. I was like a raw nerve. I went from being perfectly happy and fine to feeling as if I were hit in my solar plexus by the worst feelings. I did not say anything. I was just looking out of the bus, saying to myself, "What is going on?"

After about thirty minutes, Miguel said, "Gaya, I can't stand it. I can't stand how you are feeling." I said, "Miguel, don't help me. I can handle this myself." Those were brave words, about three o'clock in the afternoon.

That night I stayed in a room with my son. Through that long night all I could do was to keep breathing. I said a prayer to the Mother, "Please help me through this." I was aware of an energy that lived in my solar plexus. It was upside down and the color of green. It was a living being who was so contorted and so full of shame and in such emotional pain, I felt as though I were split in two, this energy and also me. I kept repeating, "I love you. Love yourself," while I tried to send this being love. At a certain point, though, I knew that this energy was going to have to redeem itself. Nothing outside of itself could ever love it enough, but I remember feeling it was a part of me.

In my work with people energetically, two things always present themselves: the inner child and the angel, or a beam of light. I thought of this place of vulnerability within myself as my inner child, in this tiny sensitive place. I was energetically dealing with all the emotions of this being inside me. This part of me had been with me through everything I had ever experienced. It knew the truth on a level that I had blocked out. I could use my defenses and not really feel my experience, but this part of me felt everything. It was experiencing my life directly with the eyes of the Judge judging itself and the eyes of the Victim being victimized by its own self-judgment.

I didn't know how this part of me would ever be able to love itself enough to forgive itself and to just be in love. I remember moving through layers of emotions. It wasn't like pictures of the past. I was feeling the pain of my being that I carried in this place. The last thing I walked through was the existential betrayal. When we are born, our divinity separates from itself so that we come into the density of matter, into our humanness, into this place of separation. To be born is a betrayal of our divinity. I saw that carrying that seed of betrayal sets up an electromagnetic system which draws to us everything based in fear and negativity. That separation, that betrayal, is the seed from which our consciousness grows and that is how we enter into fear. It is a perfect system.

Here I was with all this pain. By morning, my body was shaking. I was quivering. My heart was racing. I was very weak and I was physically fragmented.

I went over to Miguel's room and said, "I would rather die than live like this."

He said, "Do you want me to help you?"

I said, "I can't say yes, because if I do I may never have this opportunity again. What I have to tell you is that I am giving it one hundred percent and I don't care if I die."

Miguel said, "Gaya, you don't have to have a heart attack. Just remember."

I left and we prepared for the day with the group. I didn't say a word to anybody as we went to the site. Miguel walked straight to a certain rock that he had been working with for five years. He had instructed people to sit on it and absorb from it. Miguel told the group that I and the women were to go down to the rock while the men were to stay above and witness. We went down to the place in silence. I turned the rock over. When I sat on it, I felt energetically connected with the energy of the sun. Suddenly, this screaming started to move through my body. It was as though an energy were spiralling out of me and I was screaming for every woman who ever lived. I felt that the scream went to the sun. I was in such an emotional state I almost collapsed.

Then, I had a vision of the Virgin of Guadalupe. The Mother was right there. The snake that she was standing on started to grow in a swirl up her body and around her head, playing and dancing. When I saw that, I knew I had passed through a major experience. My reason did not really know what it was, but Miguel said, "Now your Parasite is redeemed because all of your pain left. You now have an Ally, but be aware to not feed any negativity to that consciousness because the Parasite will grow again. You need to love yourself and this aspect of your being. The Toltecs call this 'offering the double ethereal to the Eagle' so at death you will not lose your awareness of this lifetime."

I know now that those words meant I had passed the dragon; I had redeemed my Parasite; I had birthed my Angel. At the time I had many questions. What I have discovered is that all of life is about redemption of that aspect of your consciousness that has literally forgotten its divinity, the part that holds complete Divine consciousness and feels everything.

During the next eight months, a lot of new understandings came through to me. I went to India four months after my experience in Teo and I learned that the only place the Parasite can exist and play itself out is in resistance. It is the resistance that holds the dynamic in place within us. The deepest level of pain that I touched into was betrayal. I saw that without resistance none of this pain can be. Now I've come to the very simple place of knowing that if we don't resist, we won't poison our consciousness.

I used to talk about this when I first started my work with Miguel. He would say, "Gaya, control your emotions." That was a huge key for me. It empowered me to not be in reaction to everything, to not be an automatic computer whose button you could push and I would react in a certain way. Miguel had helped me change my point of view.

When you walk into a circumstance in life, if you have an awareness of the reaction in your body, you have a choice to either continue to react and get emotionally negative, or you can stop it. You can say to yourself, "I am a being of pure love and light. This reaction is not the truth of my nature." This is a very little thing, but once I learned about it, I began to be aware of an energy all around me.

The first time this happened I felt wings flapping around me energetically. I thought something wanted to get out, as if it were a butterfly trying to leave its cocoon. Miguel would say, "Gaya, that's you. It's the real you."

I began to realize that the essence, the driver of the car, is truly an angel. I practiced stopping my automatic reaction to life and to people. As I fed myself love and the truth of my nature, that essence became stronger and stronger in its conscious awareness. My Angel awoke.

Gaya's Lesson

When you come to life, you dream. In the dream of the two-headed snake, the head of unconsciousness eats the head of consciousness. You forget that you are Divine. You lose your divine consciousness and you forget that you are dreaming. You forget that you are God dreaming that you are not God. As you begin to define yourself from another point of view of the truth of your own nature, you see that you are love. When you recognize that you are not fear, you are Divine, you are not part of anything based in fear, then that part of you which is aware that it is Divine starts to grow.

I became aware that this energy around me was eating my emotions. Because I am a human being with a brain interacting with a soul, the purpose of my existence is to dream. My dream is the interaction between my brain and my soul, which creates my mind. The mind is emotion being eaten by energies not in human form.

Once I noticed that this energy, which is not in material form, was eating my emotions, I understood that what I really am is an angel essence. This essence stands behind me, it wraps me, it is really closer to what I am than my physical body.

You will discover that everything in the world is eating everything else, all the time. This whole realm is a feeding cycle. One thing is feeding on the other thing. It's all God eating God. This is the evolution of

God. God enters into what in this reality we call life. Life here is ruled by the sun in interaction with the earth. Divine Essence comes into this reality eating itself all the way. That energy spirals out and cycles back, with God eating God in every experience.

You are God eating God. What are you eating? You have something to say about what you are eating. You can feed yourself poison or love. What you are feeding yourself will determine which is stronger than the other, the love or the poison, and it determines where your consciousness is—in love or in poisonous fear.

As I began cleaning my mind by cleaning my wounds, I was no longer the being living inside of me torturing itself. I was empowering the angel essence of my being. As you move into love, your vibration changes. Your colors change in your auric field into finer and finer vibrations of light as you move closer to love and out of pain.

As you make this change, you are awakening your kundalini. The other head of the snake begins to awaken from its sleeping state and starts to move the Divine energy up the spinal column. You start to perceive at different levels of consciousness, which is what the chakras are. They are points of perception on particular frequency bands. If you shift your point of view into a higher vibration, you will start to perceive energy bodies that are less dense than the physical.

Each chakra has at least seven gates, and as they begin to open to other realms of perception, you experience freedom. You begin to remember that you are dreaming. At a certain place, you are on the outside of the dream. You move into love. You arrive at the place of the Mother where the love you have for everything is pure.

When I went to India, I was left with no illusions of having any being outside myself who is either loving me or judging me. I was left only with Gaya. I lost my gurus, my teachers, my guides. I lost the illusion that God is anywhere except inside of me. What is God is me because I am Divine. At first, when I was left with just myself, it was terrifying. I was raging at the stars. But I remembered that there is no way from a limited consciousness, from an intellect in a human body, that I could ever truly understand why life, which is in Divine order, seems to be filled with pain and injustice.

All I had left was the choice to choose life and every aspect of it, every human being, every circumstance, exactly the way it is and exactly the way it isn't, and to embrace it fully. If I did not do that, I would be victimized for eternity. My perception of life changed out of my choice to choose love. I see life in its perfection. I found the love of the Mother which is love without judgment. Everything is truly Divine. Everything is evolving as it needs to evolve. I found freedom. I also found the place where I trust myself absolutely. I love myself absolutely because there is nobody outside of me to judge me or to love me. Gaya is God for Gaya. It was an enormous transformation.

When I came back after that experience, I dedicated myself to the intention that every human being will remember he or she is God. This is the purpose of my life, and it has been so since childhood. I came into my realization.

The truth is we are all doing our best all of the time. You awaken when you are supposed to awaken. Free will is in how we experience the journey of life. I can choose happiness or I can choose pain. I can choose judgment or I can choose surrender.

What becomes transparent is yourself. If I do not use a defense to defend myself from feelings, I'm open. If I come into your presence and I become aware of something within myself like a feeling of sorrow or anger or righteousness, I know that is also going on with you, because we are all mirrors for each other.

We are always magnetizing to us people and circumstances for our healing, so that we can return to wholeness. If you want to see what part of you needs to come into wholeness and light, that needs to come from that place of judgment within you, look at your partner. It's amazing, but if you look outside yourself you are going to see that your circumstances constantly reflect your judgment of the places in yourself that are not healed.

When I go undefended, I am open to the experience of what I have inside of me that needs to move into wholeness. I can sense if I feel sadness, whether I am sad myself or whether I am feeling another's sadness. I can be open to the relationship instead of defending my point of view.

The Anatomy of the Parasite

The Parasite could be called the inner child. This child is pure emotion in the sense that animals are pure emotion. The Parasite feels and senses everything, without intellect. It is the sensory template of the human being. It carries all the emotional imprinting. Therefore, I could say that the human being's ability to feel is the Parasite.

I can also describe the Parasite as Lucifer, or the Challenger, or the highest angel that came into the density of matter and forgot that it is divine.

The Parasite is the child within us that screams, "Leave me alone!" At the same time, it cries, "Please, someone, come and find me. Pick me up." The message it gives itself is "I am not worthy of love. Please love me. I judge everything. I am victimized by my judgment."

In this aspect of being human, there is always the duality of the Judge and the Victim. The Parasite is the emotional body, the Fallen Angel who fell into the senses, into fields of judgment, separation, and betrayal. The Parasite is an electromagnetic force which sets up a field of fear. It is that coding inside each one of us that magnetizes into our lives similar circumstances, similar people, that always reflect what needs to be brought into wholeness. We have played this same game through many lifetimes. It is seemingly an unconscious process.

Try to imagine a diagram of a living being in which the spirit is a tiny wave of light within the soul, and they are surrounded by the body. In the space between the soul and body the interaction between body and soul creates the mind.

After the soul leaves the body, eventually, the soul will eat the mind. As the soul devours the etheric energy from the life just lived, an imprint of the etheric energy is made on the soul. The spirit then devours the soul, but the spirit retains the imprinting of etheric vibrations. We call this imprinting karma. Karma remains with the spirit as it enters a new life.

When the spirit is ready for rebirth, these traces of vibration will respond to similar vibrational patterns in the man and woman who will be the parents of the new child. Their vibrations will fit like a key in a lock of the incoming spirit.

The essence of what you are is responsible for always bringing back to you the wholeness of what you are. It pulls you into circumstances in which there are always opportunities for healing.

Karma creates holes in the soul, or the template that can only be healed by fully experiencing the feelings we have blocked through judgment. If the soul is imprinted with unresolved anger, it will come into being with parents who act out what the soul needs to heal. One parent might express anger and the other might repress it. We are using anger as our example, but we could substitute any emotional pattern.

The process by which the child is led into blocking his feelings will have these steps:

1. Memory of anger is awakened in him because he is carrying anger in his imprinting.

2. His judgment about anger is awakened, too.

3. He reacts with fear because he carries the memory of pain and judgment.

4. He closes himself to the experience by defending himself.

5. He makes a decision about anger: anger hurts. I am not able to protect myself from anger. Angry parents and angry people are dangerous. I am dangerous when I am angry. Life is not fair. It hurts me to feel.

6. The child makes an agreement: I will avoid anger. I will avoid angry people. I will avoid making people angry. I will avoid feeling angry. I will avoid feelings. Feelings are dangerous.

We are unconscious of our agreements until we actively seek them and nullify them. This work (with the silent knowledge) is so valuable because you can move beyond the agreements and heal them with awareness. Under our feelings of anger, or other emotions, there is fear. If you ask, "Where is this fear coming from?" you have the opportunity to dissolve the glue of judgment and bring it into the light. You can recapture a part of yourself that you have blocked off. The fear you feel is familiar. You experienced it under similar circumstances as a child and you made an agreement about it and we are now reacting to the fear it caused then, in the same way we did then. We are protecting ourselves according to the agreement we made in childhood. However, every time you come into awareness that you are afraid, that is where the gold is.

With awareness, we have the ability to recapture our power. We can walk back through our experiences with the eyes of love, the eyes of a loving mother and father, and heal them. We can see that it was just fear that started this defense in us. Then we realize that all our feelings and our defenses are just ourselves. I am everything both inside and outside the wall of my defense.

Our experience is just a feeling. All a feeling wants is to be felt. The solution is to feel your feelings. Once you are able to do that, the whole dynamic of the Parasite dissolves. If it is time for someone to be touched by this knowledge, it is like a wake-up call.

I know that in the 1960s, many people experienced a feeling of waking up. Something enormous happened then to the sunlight. It was supposed to occur at that time because we are always pushed by the light. The self-preoccupation that started with the social revolutions of the sixties could be the most wonderful thing that ever happened because to study the self is to study God, the Divine, the Real Self, not the ego self.

The same consciousness of spirit that provoked the spiritual quests of the sixties is still choosing. The spirit that chose your circumstances, your parents, and your life is still choosing whatever is coming into your life right now. We think we are doing the choosing, but we are always returning to wholeness. We get there by experiencing life just as it is and just as it is not, without judgment. We do not do it with our mind or the Parasite. We just enter a place of no judgment and that is what

surrender is. We accept that everything is divinely perfect and we surrender to the experience. We call this passing the dragon.

I have passed the dragon. I never have to pass it again. To get outside
the dream, to pass the dragon into the pure black light, I had to fight
for it. Our auric field protects us from the black light. Pure black light
is not conducive to life. Therefore, passing the dragon involves physical
risk. It is easier for women to pass the dragon in some ways because we
know how to surrender. Surrender is encoded within women because
they are required to let go of their children physically at birth, and later,
they must release them emotionally.

Gaya's Dream

In my dream, I learned that there is nothing to see in spirit because
there is no form to it. All of a sudden, I saw a little piece of something
that looked like netting. It had a shape that I recognized as a piece of
film moving like a wave. As it bumped into the place in my dream that
was spirit, a little light went on inside. The image was like a film with
a light, but it was only a reflection.

I knew that I was looking at the mind, the manifesting element of the
spirit, the mother, that aspect of creation that can reproduce itself. From
the marriage of the spirit and the film with the light in it, a multiplication
began that soon built a whole new world. Buried down inside it was
still that little ray of light that is found in each human being. This is the
divine energy that is trapped within the spinal column, the sleeping angel.

The truth is that we are THAT. We are spirit, which is no thing, it
has no form. It is that which we can never know. We can only know
life in reflection, which is MIND, the moon. It is not the light itself.
The true nature of reflection is separation and duality.

The mind, the reflection, is always looking for itself. If we function and
process life from the point of view of the mind only, we can therefore
never find our true self because it is only the reflection of the light. It
is caught in the duality of separation. All that we see in reality is mind.
The truth of its nature is illusion.

Angels

When I became aware of the energetic that was eating my emotions, I made a commitment that I would only feed it love. I try to the best of my ability to feed this energy angel nothing but love.

We need to "jump the track" to the point of view of the angel. The angel's viewpoint gives us a lot more space to witness the personality that we are in this life. I can see that Gaya has always done her best. She makes mistakes, but I have great compassion for her because I am no longer jammed into her. I am so thankful that, through her, I can experience life. She is my car, my vehicle in which I am experiencing life. I can love her absolutely.

In my dream, when I saw the reflection of the light, I saw it as a movie. I knew that life is like a holographic movie. I am the producer and the director and I'm constantly making images to serve my movie. I am casting you to fit into a role in my movie. I am always projecting my image which then reflects myself back to me like a closed circuit TV screen.

From a spiritual point of view, you can come to every circumstance with the eyes of the angel or the dreamer seeing the movie being played. This is not possible from the mental point of view. The mind can never understand itself ("It" is the object world; "Self" is the Divine) because it is trapped in duality.

With faith that all is divinely perfect, you can choose to express your life from a place of ultimate responsibility as your angel rather than the Judge or the Parasite. Life is perfect all the time. You are an angel working in this dimension, evolving the human being you call yourself. Wake up from the dream and know you are dreaming. You are Divine. Angels belong in heaven. Come home.

Be: Feel what there is to feel.

Do: Practice the art of stalking and transformation. Remember your commitment to love yourself.

Have: Live a self-actualizing experience of life. You recapture yourself every time you break the dynamic of the Parasite feeding itself poison.

The Rule of the Nagual

The chakras (from the Hindu tradition) are spinning points of perception in our spiritual body that we associate with areas of our physical body. The seven traditional chakra centers are found at the base of the spine, the gonads, the solar plexus, the heart, the throat, the forehead, and the crown of the head.

Gaya believes that each chakra represents an angel. Lucifer, the Challenger, who guards the lower chakras at the base of the spine and the gonads, is both the Parasite and pure love. The Parasite is the separation of Divinity into mind. Gaya describes the separation from the divine by the descent into matter at birth as a form of betrayal. In our myths, Lucifer is the twin or the opposite of Ariel. Lucifer represents the dark and Ariel the light, but both are of God and therefore both are pure love.

The third chakra is at the solar plexus and the Tree of Death.

It is guarded by Ariel, a name meaning Guardian.

Raphael guards the fourth chakra at the heart. There is a large jump in perception at the heart chakra. Masters live and resonate at the heart level, but they move into the higher chakras when they perform miracles. Below the heart is the survival level of vibration. Above the heart is mind seeking itself.

The fifth chakra is at the throat, which is the place of communication. Gabriel, the Messenger, guards the throat, the Word.

The sixth chakra is the upper mind and it is guarded by Michael who fights the dragon of the Parasite.

The seventh chakra is the Tree of Life at the crown of the head. This is the chakra of illumination. Here, Ariel again stands guard.

The chakra system is represented in its entirety by the snake.

Gaya says, "To go back up the Tree of Life is to return to the Divine." In the Indian tradition, the kundalini is the energy of the snake rising up the spine into illumination.

Gaya speaks of the pure essence as the black light of the sun.

"It is the purest light we know. It is where creation comes from. Our whole purpose in being here in life is to get back to this black light of pure essence."

Each time the soul takes a body and develops a mind, trapped inside us is a little trapped black light. This light is wrapped in the soul, and it goes on lifetime after lifetime until it gets back to its purest form.

At the moment of your birth, just as you emerged from your mother, your pineal gland was penetrated by a ray of light from a waving band of archangel energy above the earth. This ray entering your pineal gland determined which archangel would be your guardian in this life. Your essence is that of an archangel, also. These two angels are not necessarily the same energy. You therefore carry two angel energies, that of your essence and that of your guardian angel. To separate the two angels, Gaya speaks of the guardian as the "little angel."

As you build your mind in childhood, you are also building the first filter around your little guardian archangel. This covering fits over the angel in the same way the soul covers the spirit. Beneath this filter, your guardian angel is apparently asleep and forgetting that it is an angel.

"This covering of the angel is what we call the Parasite. It lives within the mind and it is ruled by the reason," Gaya teaches.

By waking up, you are making holes in the covering of your archangel, through which you are exposed more and more to the black light of your real Self. At some point in the cleansing process when you reach a high vibration of love, the guardian archangel jumps through its covering and mates with your essence or primary archangel.

It is the mating of your guardian angel and your permanent angel essence that takes you back to God. This is what I call the Reproduction of the Angels and the Rule of the Nagual. You are an angel in evolution. Your angel is evolving humanity. From this mating, the birth of the angel happens and you return to your Divine Self. You will never be pulled back into the earthly life again because your vibration will be the same as God's, pure Divinity.

From my experience, I am still a physical human being but the personality called Gaya is gone. The way she expresses herself is completely different. I always wanted to be behind the scenes. Now I take responsibility for my expression. Now is the time. That is why I am talking now.

Once you get out of the box, out of the dream, you cannot fit back into the box of reasonable explanations. You expand immeasurably. I am no longer contained. Everything is *love*.

I carry a lot of energy because I no longer waste my energy reacting to everything in life. My personal importance is not eating up all my energy. I can use my energy to move your Assemblage Point by my intent. The way I do that is by moving my own. I live in the Oneness. This is not a matter of intellect. It cannot be understood by the mind. This is my Angel driving my car, my personality.

How to Enter the Realm of Magic

After you have begun to understand the anatomy of the Parasite, there are ways that you can assist your progress into the realm of magic, or the path of transcendence. Moment by moment, rather than at a separate time during which you are practicing stalking, you can live consciously and remember these two concepts:

1. You can dissolve your defense systems by noticing when you feel a resistance and by immediately letting go of it. If you feel an uncomfortableness, embrace it. That is the way home. Feel what you are feeling. Honor yourself there. See the consequences of your actions and choose from the highest place of awareness.

2. Love yourself. Lose your feeling that you are living for others' approval. Put the love of yourself in first place and honor it always. In those tender, vulnerable places within your being, there is a voice. It needs to express itself. It needs to be honored.

Resistance feeds the Parasite. If you are in a conversation and you feel you are resisting someone else's words, say to yourself, "I don't need to do this." This is a mastery in and of itself. I am talking about being present in the moment with yourself. If you are aware, you can make the choice not to resist by saying, "Right now, I choose not to react. I am a loving being of pure light and anything other than that is simply a reflection of an illusion." Just doing that changes your vibration from the survival level to the fourth chakra. It is *magic.*

Usually, there are two basic dynamics which arouse resistance. One is, "Don't tell me what to do." The other is the fear of being cheated. In the domestication process, our parents told us to "stop being so naive; the world will eat you alive; it's dog-eat-dog out there." We were prepared to be be afraid of being cheated. When you feel afraid, you can ask yourself if you are afraid of being told what to do, or of being cheated. These are two main responses that destroy trust. Always having to be right is the mind's tool of survival. If you are right, then I'm wrong. I don't exist.

You have within yourself the power, every second, to transform your experience. That is where the magic is. The key to magic is self-awareness.

You are the magician. First you become aware. Then you shift your point of view.

We spend so much energy trying to be in control. Think about it. We are bubbles of perception, living on the earth, the core of which is molten lava spinning in space. Yet, we carry the illusion that we can be in control. The only thing we can control is our reaction to life and how we choose to experience the journey. When we stop trying to control everything—which is an illusion anyway—we can be a bubble floating on the river, around the rocks, in perfect harmony. Life becomes so beautiful.

A Personal Message

Words cannot touch the depth of love, respect, and gratitude I hold in my heart for Miguel. Through his teachings and the demonstration of his ever-constant impeccability, I've learned to live a life worth living . . . a life unguarded in which I walk unafraid and open to the experiences life presents to me.

Miguel showed me that if you let the power of love flow through you, there is nothing from which you need to protect yourself. Through his eyes, I began to see the light in everyone and everything, which opened me to a path of freedom, the freedom to be true to myself, to express my truth no matter what that may look like to anyone else.

I've learned you can never really say "yes" when you don't have the ability to say "no." In that, I've found the way to truly give, not from a place of need but from the place of love that holds no separation, no expectations, no attachments, and is boundless in expression.

To the Nagual, I say, thank you for the gifts of the sun, the moon, and the stars ever dancing in the glow of the eternal divine flame that lives within all of us. I love you.

Miguel Interprets Gaya's Story

Miguel Ruiz:

When I met Gaya, I recognized what she really is. I could see all the wisdom that comes into that body and mind. I also saw how she limits herself. I saw how she used all her wisdom and intelligence to express her fear of taking responsiblity for what she knows.

For years I worked with her to break the agreements she had made that limited her. Gradually, she was changing.

She would have a great idea and give it to someone else to carry out because she did not want to do it. She tried to justify her own divinity in someone else's divinity. She recognized God in Sai Baba and Premananda, but not in herself.

In 1994, I saw an opportunity to challenge all Gaya's beliefs. I put her in a place of emptiness where she was face to face with God. I took away her comfort level where she felt safe and where she had someone else to make her feel safe. It took her a long time to digest that.

We went to Mexico and we were traveling from San Miguel de Allende to Teotihuacán by bus. Gaya asked me, "Help me to be myself . . . entirely." I asked her if she truly meant it. I asked her three times. Each time, she said, "Yes, please."

As an act of power with my will, I took away her defenses. She saw herself exactly. I pulled out of her energy field her denial system. It uncovered her wounds. I did not say a word about it. Soon, I could feel her emotional pain. Her pain was so great, I asked her if she wanted help, or to stop. She said, "No."

We arrived in Teotihuacán and we each had our own room. She had the worst night of her life. I felt it. It seemed too much. I felt that maybe she needed me to have me put back her denial system. At one point, she felt it would be better to die than to continue the way she was.

The next morning, I took her to the Place of the Air. I have prepared a rock there for my apprentices. Gaya sat on the rock and she received the Redemption. In five or ten very intense minutes she healed all her wounds and she forgave herself. The Parasite redeemed itself and became an Ally. Remember that the Parasite is the combination of the Judge and the Victim. The Parasite had always sabotaged everything Gaya did. Now the Parasite no longer eats fear. Now it pushes her mind to create love.

The transformation of Gaya began there and it ended in India when she went to see Premananda later in the year. In India, Gaya found her voice. Now, with all her humility she accepts her divinity and she teaches others.

CHAPTER THIRTEEN

PROPHECIES

Human beings have always been aware of their own mortality and they have craved to know the future. Every age has had its prophets and its prophecies. Prophecies worldwide and in all time periods have agreed in one fundamental way: they are about the evolution of the human species.

In this chapter, Miguel will recapitulate the Toltec's silent knowledge as he leads the reader toward a summation in prophecy. His central thesis is that all humans together form one living being, which is an organ of Planet Earth. Each human is to the earth what a single cell is to a human body. Cells live and die continuously in our body. In the same way, humans are born, they mature, and they die. The constant replenishment of humans keeps the human organ of the earth alive, just as new cells keep the human body alive. We are observing, on different time scales, the same process of physical life giving way to physical death throughout the universe.

Miguel Ruiz:

Humans are multidimensional in matter, multidimensional in the mind, multidimensional in the soul, and unidimensional in spirit. In matter, we find that our bodies are made by billions and billions of little living beings that we call cells. Every cell is an individual that we can take out of our body, put in the laboratory and it will stay alive, yet it will continue to be part of our body.

A liver cell has no awareness that it is part of a whole being with an awareness of itself as "I am." It does not know that, together with all the other cells in the liver, the brain, the heart, the bones, and all the cells throughout the body, it helps to form this single living being.

A single human being is one part of the organ that is humanity. The totality of all humans forms one organ of the Planet Earth. Planet Earth is alive and it has its own metabolism. There are many organs in this beautiful living being. The atmosphere is an organ. The oceans are an organ. The forests are an organ. All the animals are an organ. And we are all that they are. We are the air. We are the oceans. We are all the animals that exist on Planet Earth. And we have communication with the other organs in the same way that the liver can communicate with the heart and with the brain.

Extending further, we can see that the Planet Earth is both a living being and also an organ in the solar system, with the sun at the center and all the planets, the moons, and other satellites in orbit around the sun. The solar system is also one living being that is ruled by the sun.

The solar system that is one living being is, at the same time, just a piece of the gigantic being that is the universe.

A single atom with its electrons in orbit around its nucleus is another solar system. The atom and the solar system are therefore analogous. Our body is composed of billions of atoms, each one a miniature solar system. In the universe, there are billions upon billions of stars, each a living being, and together they form just one living being. The Toltecs knew of these analogies and similarities reflected in different realities throughout the universe.

The big questions—who are we? where did we come from? where are we going?—are resolved in the Toltec point of view, which is that we are everything there is. One small human body is a single piece of a chain within that huge biological machine that is the universe. This chain has communication with everything that exists in the whole universe.

Although this explanation satisfies the material point of view of our eyes and our ears, something must be added to it because we are not just matter. What about how we feel? What about anger, jealousy, sadness, happiness, and love? These aspects of our human life are evidence of an energy other than the material. We call this ethereal energy.

Energy is alive. Everything that exists is alive. Ethereal energy is also a living being. Ethereal energy includes our emotions. Our emotions are alive. Our thinking is alive. All of our feelings are alive, and they are us. Our mind is creating billions of emotions. In the same way that our cells create our body, our emotions create our mind. Therefore our mind is made of ethereal energy. Remember that the function of our mind is to dream. We dream twenty-four hours a day. We dream when we are awake and we dream when we are sleeping. We dream with our mind, not with our brain. Yet, the brain knows that the mind is dreaming.

All human minds together are an organ of the Planet Earth, but this organ exists in a different dimension from that of our bodies. Our bodies are part of the material dimension which we can touch. Our minds exist in the ethereal dimension of thought and feelings. In the same way that all of our emotions together create an individual mind, all minds together create the mind of the Planet Earth, and that mind is dreaming, too. This collective dream is composed of all the individual dreams each of us is dreaming. The collective dream includes the dreams of the family, the dreams of the community, of the city, of the state, of the country, of the whole continent, and finally, the dream of the whole planet.

At each level of dreaming, there are distinct differences in the dream. For example, if we visit another country, we will find that its dream is different from that of our own country, and it is alive. The dream in China is different from the one in Persia, but there is something in common in the dreams. People everywhere suffer. People struggle. In their interactions, people everywhere spread poison. This is an ethereal poison, not a physical one, but the poison affects the physical body. The poison we call anger, hate, sadness, jealousy, shyness, all come from the same thing that controls the dream of the planet—and this is fear. Fear is the big demon, the big devil in the dream of the planet. Our interactions with each other are based on fear, human to human, society to society, nation to nation. The way we dream is self-destructive. We are destroying ourselves as individuals and as a society.

No matter where we go, we will find that people have a Judge and a Victim in their minds. They all find guilt in themselves and in other people. When we feel guilty, we have a need to be punished. When others are guilty, we need to punish them.

The Victim is that part of the mind that says, "Poor me. I'm not good enough. I'm not strong enough. I'm not intelligent enough. How can I survive? Why should I try? I'm just a human." So, every step is fearful. That is the way humans dream. With this review of Toltec silent knowledge, we can see that the dream has to change. Prophecies are about changing the dream. Around the world, all prophecies are coming true at the same time, right at this time. Now!

We are reminded that this living being of Planet Earth is controlled by the sun. The earth is an organ of the sun. All decisions for the metabolism of the planet come from the sun. The sun controls the earth through its messengers. In the Judeo-Christian tradition, these are called angels. Well, the messenger is nothing but the light of the sun. Everything that exists in the whole universe is nothing but energy, and that energy is light.

Our body is light, but it is condensed light. Our mind is light. Our soul is light in different manifestations. Light perceives light in any of the directions. This is why we can perceive with the eyes, but we also can perceive with the mind, with the soul, and with the spirit.

What is the spirit? I call it Intent. Intent, spirit, God . . . these are names for the same energy. A property of this energy is that it makes possible any change, any transformation. God is intent. God is spirit. God is God. God is light. God is the real you. God is the real me.

Energy or light is the first manifestation of intent, or the first manifestation of God, or of the spirit. Everything is alive because of God, because of you. You are not your body. You are not your cells. You are not your mind. You are not your soul. You are light. You are life.

Without you, your body will just collapse. Without you, your soul will collapse. Your essence is light. Light is everywhere.

Light is alive and it is a living being. The light carries all the information for any kind of life on Planet Earth. There are billions of different vibrations of light. Mother Earth transforms whatever information comes in the light from the Father Sun to create life. The DNA in each of our cells is a ray from the sun trapped by the Mother Earth and condensed into matter.

All knowledge that exists is in the light. Light is the way stars communicate from one to the other, just as light is the way one atom communicates with another atom.

Change comes according to our perception. We see light streaming like a river from the sun. Like a river it is always the same form, but the energy is always different. If we shift our point of view slightly, this river of light will look solid. It will fill the whole space between the stars just like a nerve system.

Whatever happens anywhere in the universe will be known by the whole universe because the communication is instantaneous. In our material point of view, the speed of light is 186,000 miles per second, which we think is probably the fastest speed possible, but actually there is a quality in the light that is thousands of times faster than our measurements. It is this quality that allows for instant communication across the universe.

Everything we perceive, in the material world, is a light that enters our eyes as a reflection from objects. We do not actually see an object. We are dreaming what we see. We create the entire reality in our minds.

In our dream, what we think of as matter I call the frame of the dream. The frame is the same for everybody. We dream with the same frame. The frame gives us the direction of time and space. It makes us feel safe.

As soon as we interpret what we are seeing, we find that each of us makes a different interpretation because we dream a different dream. Each of us has our own dream based on everything that we believe.

To illustrate this idea, think of a thousand new computers exactly alike, each completely blank, without information. As soon as we put information into these computers, each will be different.

This is what happens with human beings. Our mind is a biological machine like a computer. There is different information in every human being according to the person's experience. Each one has learned differently from parents, society, school, and religion. The information that we put in our computer is what will teach us to dream. It tells us how to interpret what we perceive.

Each human computer has a name, but a name is only an agreement we have made. I am not really a human being named Miguel Angel. You are not a human being either. We just agree that we are humans. Everything that we put in our computers is an agreement. It is not necessarily good or bad, right or wrong. It is just information. According to that information, we perceive the world and call it reality. This information is the source of our limitations. We create images about ourselves and about everything else. We then want to believe in those images. The process of putting the information in the computer is the Domestication.

We are all animals that were domesticated by other animals, other humans. We were domesticated in the same way that we domesticate dogs, by punishment and reward. We domesticate our children the way we were domesticated. We are afraid to be punished and we are afraid to not get the reward. We create images of ourselves designed to please others. We want to be good enough to please mom and dad, the teacher, society, the church, and God. Our behavior depends upon the image we have created about ourselves, with all those limitations. What others think about us is very important to us. We guide our lives with reference to others' opinions. We try to please everybody else, rather than ourselves.

The dream of the planet, held by all of us, is the same. When we rise out of the dream of the planet and out of our own dream, we find that what we have thought of as truth is nothing but information in our computer and it can easily be changed. We resist change because we are afraid. Fear controls our life. Fear controls our dream. The evolution of humanity is the evolution of fear in the Planet Earth.

From outside the planet, we can see that evolution of the whole human race is akin to the life of a single living being who is born, grows and reproduces, and will transform. Everything is indestructible really. It does not die. It transforms.

The progress of evolution has a certain logic. The living being of all humans combined will undergo changes in the same way that a single human changes. Imagine a young girl, eleven years of age. She will soon have her first period and become a woman. When some of the organs in this little woman change, that information is known by the brain and the brain will push other organs to create certain kinds of hormones that will complete the cycle. The process will be controlled by the brain.

The maturation process of the woman is comparable to that of the human race as a whole. When certain transformations of body, mind, and soul occur in some humans, the sun, via light messengers, will know and the sun will change the quality of the light it transmits, sending a different message to the human organ of the earth. In turn, this change will cause the whole of humanity to change.

At this time humans are finally leaving their childhood and becoming mature. They have more clarity. Their reason is surrendering to their intuition. Their way of dreaming is changing. Fear was necessary to promote the growth of reason and the mind. Reason prepared the mind for intuition.

Human beings are multidimensional. In addition to the body and the mind, we are all formed of light from the sun. The real core of a human being is a personal ray of light in connection with the sun. Therefore, whatever happens in the single human is known by the sun through this light. Any change occuring in a single human affects the sun and its response affects the rest of humanity. This is the process of human evolution.

Once we find our personal ray of light, we can shift our point of view to the sun and see the human race all at once. I teach my apprentices to find that ray of light connecting them to the sun. When they can do this, the silent knowledge enters their mind and they just know, without thought or fear. Humans who can do this are prophets who point the way for others.

Today we are becoming mutants, because our mind is changing. We are aware that we are dreaming and we are controlling our dream. Automatically, we are rejecting one quality of light and accepting another; as we do this, we are modifying our connection to the sun. We do not need to work for it to happen. It is occurring already. The sun controls earth life from the virus to the dinosaur to the human. All modifications come from the sun.

The sun is enormously more intelligent than any of us. It has supreme intelligence. Humans all over the world have recognized this. Ancient Egyptians worshipped Ra, the sun god. In Teotihuacán, they also knew that the sun controls the earth. They were aware that at certain intervals, life on this planet changed when the sun changed. According to the Toltec calendar—which is also the Mayan and Aztec calendar—there have been five suns prior to the one that exists now. Their prophecies said that there would be a huge earthquake in Mexico's biggest city of Tenochtitlan. On September 19, 1985, this earthquake struck Mexico City, which is the modern Tenochtitlan. The ancient Toltecs predicted that after the earthquake there would be a period of rest until the new sun was born. On January 11, 1992, the new sun came, and it has sparked a great change in all humans.

The Sixth Sun has a different quality of light and it will transform the dream of the planet. It will transform the human mind, making it more aware of itself as a light being connected to the sun. As an individual, you will speed your own evolution if you just open to yourself and who you really are.

All the masters on earth are trying to tell you the same thing, and this is that you have something wonderful inside of you which you can open to. The mind is a living being. The mind eats and digests the emotions which come through ideas. As more and more masters speak of the silent knowledge, more and more humans will ingest these ideas. The ideas will transform the information in their computers and give them a chance for a better life.

This is the prophecy for the next humanity. Human beings will know who they are. They will communicate with each other. They will love each other. They will stop judging and they will control the dream. They will be happy.

When Jesus tried to explain all of these things 2,000 years ago, he spoke of a new way to see God. They killed him. At this time, we are ready to hear these truths.

We think we are the most intelligent species on earth, but we are only a small piece of intelligence. The ideas that we think are our own are really already in existence when we become aware of them and think that we "think" them. As we transform, we will perceive ideas directly from where they are stored in nature. I experienced this in Teotihuacán when I understood the knowledge and the images stored there in the rocks.

Once we are aware that we are directly connected to the sun, we can suggest a behavior to another of earth's organs. This is the way that shamans control the rain. They do not do so with their reason, but with their intuition. Reason will not connect because it does not believe in itself. Intuition connects you to your personal ray of light. This is why prayer is so powerful when we expect to have an answer. Usually, the answer to our prayer is not what the reason expects.

When we connect and witness in a shamanic way, it is not our personality that brings about changes. The sun does. It was not the little Jesus personality who changed water into wine, nor was it Moses who divided the waters of the Red Sea. It was the will of the sun that did those things. For the sun, everything is possible.

It is the same for each of us. We do not need to expect what happens. We do not need to make something happen. We ask and we witness. The sun, with its superior intelligence, will create the answer. How can we doubt our personal destiny? There is no place for doubts anymore.

The prophets said that when the Sixth Sun came, God would awaken from the dream. This means that we are God dreaming that we are not God. Although it will take at least two hundred years for the process of awakening to be completed, since 1992 the process has been accelerating. This generation is the one that is beginning the awakening and you are a part of it.

What we need to do is surrender to our destiny. Whatever happens will happen because it must. Our task is to enjoy our life more and to express what is inside of us to bring about the new humanity. If we have hate inside of us, we share hate. If we have sadness, we share sadness. You can only share happiness when you are happy. You cannot share love unless you love yourself first.

The dream of the planet will not change without resistance, just as we cannot change our own dream without experiencing resistance. The new dream is already here and growing, but the old dream wants to hang onto guilt, anger, the Judge, and the Victim. The human pattern of spiritual growth is like an inner war where we face ourselves. We are the most severe judge of ourselves.

Each of us will go through a crisis of surrender, but afterwards our capacity to love will increase. The Parasite who lives inside our mind, constantly trying to undermine our progress with emotional poison, will gradually give up and become our Ally. As it happens in the individual, it will also happen in all of humanity.

All of our prophetic books describe the resistance of the dream of the planet during the time of change. The prediction of horrors relates to the fears released by resistance to change. During the last fifty years, the human race has tried to destroy itself with fear, but it has failed. Especially during the last fifteen years, humanity has been in chaos, but the old dream is already broken and resistance is lessening.

In the Book of Revelation, in the Bible, John speaks of the Seven Seals. At the time of his writing, letters were sealed with wax. The seal had to be broken in order to read the information inside. That is symbolic. Every seal that is broken in the Book of Revelation increases our awareness of the modifications coming into the earth via light from the sun.

There is no reason to fear. Even if our body dies in some predicted disaster, we have no reason to fear. It will die anyway. Do not listen to prophets of fear. Don't be guided by them. The old dream of the planet is using many channels to create fear. Even the gods are trying to create fear and panic, because the gods eat human emotions and they crave them. Jesus, Buddha, and Sai Baba, the contemporary holy man in India, have lived lives without fear. They did not cause fanaticism. Their lives were their messages more than their words.

The next two hundred years will be a time of growth, with the transformation moving faster and faster. There will then be a period of at least three or four thousand years of peace until a new cycle begins. A dream is biological. It is born, it transforms, and it dies.

The story of evolution repeats itself like a spiral, rising higher and higher, then it goes downward again. Life, too, goes in cycles. When you know these cycles, you can predict what will happen. You need only know what stage of evolution we are in now to be able to see the future. We are now in a major period of transition.

There are three parts to the cyclic pattern of the dream of humanity. In part one, which is the darkest time, reason controls the dream. In the second stage, reason and instinct, or intuition, are mixed. This leads to a fast period of growth and transformation. In the last stage, destruction occurs in order to rebuild the dream. Today, we are almost at the end of that part of the cycle in which reason and intuition are mixed. Intuition is going to rule the next period. Intuition is about trusting. It is knowing without thinking, without doubt. This is where we are in the cycle. Reason, which controls a false dream, has transformed now to intuition for those who are already changed.

Far ahead of us, beyond the present cycle, there will be another period of reason. Those we now call human will live in a different part of the universe. Those who remain here will have a new sort of energy. I do not think the humans of that time will be like us. I believe they will live in the oceans. Today there are two species living in the oceans who are starting to dream as humans. What will make the difference in the coming transformation is not the physical form but what is created in the mind. The importance to us of these prophecies is that we are already transforming. We are mutants.

Love is becoming the biggest transformation in the human world. For thousands of years, humans repressed love. They forgot what love means.

When we say, "I need you," that is not love. That is possessiveness. If we feel jealousy and we want to control another, that is not real love. Possessive love is like any other need of the human body. Imagine going without food for a week. You would feel as though you were starving. Then if someone gave you a taste of bread, you would feel, "I need this bread. I love this bread." Falling in love is something like that.

When we were children under four years of age, our emotional body was made to perceive love. Then, domestication began and fear began. Fear took the place of love. Every time we started to express our love, something in us repressed it. We felt hurt and then we became afraid to love. We limited our love to just a few people. With others, we would say, "I love you, IF . . ." This meant, "I will love you, if you let me control you." That kind of love creates a strong dependency, just like a drug.

In a human relationship, one partner often has more need for love than the other and that partner gives power to the other. This is like the relationship between a drug addict and the supplier. The one who gives the drug is in complete control and can manipulate the other person through fear. A broken heart is like a drug addict who cannot secure the drug. It causes the same emotions. It is very common to be scared to love because for a small pleasure there is such a large payment.

During the last fifty years, marriage has changed so much that it has almost been destroyed. It had to happen as part of the process of cleansing that all the emotions and fears in marriage had to be released. Marriage will be re-created without the need to control another person. It will be based on respect. A woman will have the right to be one hundred percent woman. A man will have the right to be a one hundred percent man.

When we respect each other's dream, there is no conflict. When we are not afraid to love, when we do not stipulate conditions for our love, everything will change. Today, there is little respect. As soon as I tell you what to do, that means I do not respect you. Feeling sorry for someone shows a lack of respect. Feeling sorry is not compassionate. Feeling sorry for someone else awakens our own self-pity. If I feel sorry for you, it means that I think you are not strong enough or intelligent enough to make it. If you feel sorry for me, you do not respect me or think that I am intelligent or strong enough to make it. When we try to do something for somebody else, this shows lack of respect. Having compassion is seeing that someone has fallen, helping that person to stand up, and then saying "yes," he or she can do it.

Even though people might be in the worst conditions, we do not need to feel sorry for them. We need to love them. We can help them with our compassion. A person can always choose. What has happened to the person happened because of choices he or she made.

Humans will recover their sense of responsibility. For centuries, we have tried to avoid responsiblity, yet whatever we do always causes a reaction. We cannot escape cause and effect. We do not need to take responsibility for another's mistakes. We can help and give love, but we do not need to take responsiblity for others because that encourages their illusion of avoiding responsiblity. This applies even to our children, spouses, and parents or friends. If we take on their responsibilities, they become weak.

Action is what makes the difference in this reality. The power is in the action, not in the dream. Through your actions, you have the power to change everything. You can claim the freedom to act on behalf of transformation.

On one of my shamanic journeys, I learned that knowledge is a limitation, a barrier to freedom. Knowledge is only a description of the dream. Everything that we know is describing what we dream. And, what we dream is not real. So, knowledge is not real. Yet, knowledge seems valuable because we use it to communicate and interchange our ideas and our emotions. The problem is that if we put all the knowledge we have accumulated into our personal computer and base our actions on it, knowledge will prevent us from transcending. Knowledge tries to convince our reason that transcendence is not possible.

I tell my apprentices that knowledge is the last barrier of the warrior. We accumulate knowledge only to change the information in our computer. Once we change and become who we really are, we no longer need knowledge. You need to cross the river of knowledge in order to transcend and not come back here anymore.

Our knowledge closes off our intuition. Intuition leads us to the truth. Truth is alive. Everything is in evolution. Everything is biological. Everything is alive.

Your only responsibility in this life is to make yourself happy. We do not need knowledge for that, because everything we require is already here. Other peoples' love can awaken your love, but it is your own love that makes you happy. That love is your own truth. It is your freedom.

The best way to take advantage of the change that is in process is to stop resisting it. We are not here to please others. We are here to please ourselves. You can do whatever you want. If you focus your intent, there is no doubt that you will get what you want. This is true for everyone.

The Toltecs were the supreme artists of the Americas. They expressed their sense of beauty with great skill in all ways. All humans are artists and the art they are creating is their personal dream. As you awaken to the silent knowledge, you can ask yourself, "How beautiful is my life? How much do I love? How well do I communicate? How happy am I?"

I encourage you to be the supreme artist of your personal dream. Make it as beautiful as possible. Express your beauty.

THE CAVE OF
THE BEST WARRIOR

There was once a very strong and very tall man who used to be a soldier. He called himself the Best Warrior. He was in many wars and he killed a lot of people. In his little nation, he was a hero. Everyone feared him and respected him. Whatever he wanted to do, he did because no one would stop him. Wherever he went, he would say, "I am the Best Warrior."

One day, the soldier was claiming he was the Best Warrior when a little boy said, "I don't think you are the Best Warrior."

The soldier was infuriated. He picked up the child and said, "You are lucky to be a child because many people have died for less than that. If I am not the best, who do you think is the Best Warrior?"

The child replied, "In the middle of the jungle, in a cave, is a man and he is really the Best Warrior."

The soldier went into the jungle immediately to look for his rival. He wanted to kill him. Finally, he found the cave and he called out a challenge.

"Come out and fight me and we will see who is the Best Warrior." Imagine his surprise when an old man stepped out of the cave. The old man was so weak, he could hardly walk.

The soldier laughed. "Somebody has played a trick on me. Someone told me you are the Best Warrior."

With very kind eyes, the old man said, "Whoever told you that spoke the truth. I am the Best Warrior."

"First a little boy. Now an old man. I don't want to have to kill you."

"If you did, that would only prove you are a murderer, not a warrior. I don't think you have the courage to live alone, like me, in the jungle," said the old man.

"Hmmm," answered the soldier.

"I challenge you to live one whole year in this jungle. After a year, come to see me again and let's see who is the Best Warrior."

The soldier accepted the challenge and he lived for a whole year in the jungle. He became a great hunter. He learned from the eagle. He learned from the jaguar. And, he learned from the spider.

After that year, he went back to see the old man. Again, the old man challenged him to stay another year and to use all the techniques he had learned about hunting to hunt for knowledge. "After a year of hunting knowledge, come to see me again and let's see who is the Best Warrior."

Using the techniques of the hunter, of the eagle, the jaguar, and the spider, the soldier learned everything about nature, about the stars, the animals, and mathematics. He accumulated a lot of knowledge and the more he learned, the greater his ego grew. He said to himself, "There is no doubt. I am the BEST."

When he saw the old man again, the old man challenged him to stay another year hunting himself. The soldier accepted the challenge.

He began hunting every emotion, every action, every reaction that he had. He started to see himself and to face himself. He struggled with his belief system. He started accepting everything and loving himself. The transformation was so amazing that in a very short time, only three months of hunting himself, he really felt that the old man was his master, his teacher, and truly the Best Warrior. He felt so much love for the old man. And he felt compassion for all the people he had hurt. He could hardly wait to see the old man again, so he went back to the cave and called out to him.

But the old man did not come from the cave. Hesitantly, the soldier stepped into the cave and all he found was an empty body. The old man had died.

Then, the soldier decided he would stay in that cave and become the Best Warrior.

He is right there in that cave now, waiting for your challenge.

Thank you for reading my words and for letting me love you as you really are, a light being connected to the sun by your personal ray of sunlight, a being who is also God. I love you.

~ MIGUEL ANGEL RUIZ